# Hoops!

# Hoops!

© Brian Drake

## HIGHLIGHTS, HISTORY, AND STARS

## GREG GARBER

### FRIEDMAN/FAIRFAX
### PUBLISHERS

**A FRIEDMAN/FAIRFAX BOOK**

ISBN 1-56799-060-6

Editors: Sharon Kalman and Kelly Matthews
Art Director: Jeff Batzli
Designer: Kevin Ullrich
Photography Editor: Anne K. Price

Typeset by Trufont
Color separations by United South Sea Graphic Art Co.
Printed and bound in China by Leefung-Asco Printers Ltd.

The publisher wishes to acknowledge that extensive attempts have been made to ensure that this book be as accurate and up to date as possible at press time.

For bulk purchases and special sales, please contact:
Friedman/Fairfax Publishers
15 West 26 Street
New York, NY 10010
212/685-6610 FAX 212/685-1307

# DEDICATION

For Christopher Gregory Garber

# ACKNOWLEDGMENTS

Sincere thanks to those who helped bring this book to life: my understanding family, Gerry, Emily, and Christopher; all the terrific players who gave their time and insight; Wayne R. Patterson of the Basketball Hall of Fame; the National Basketball Association; the National Collegiate Athletic Association; Mike Arace and Peter May, rabid hoopologists for the Hartford *Courant* and Boston *Globe*; Jim Russell of the Indianapolis *News*; and Jeffrey Twiss of the Boston Celtics.

# CONTENTS

I N T R O D U C T I O N

page 8

C H A P T E R  O N E

THE EVOLUTION OF
BASKETBALL

page 16

C H A P T E R  T W O

THE POSITIONS

page 36

C H A P T E R  T H R E E

THE PRO GAME

page 74

C H A P T E R  F O U R

THE COLLEGE GAME

page 98

STATISTICS

page 120

SELECTED MEMORABLE
EVENTS IN BASKETBALL
HISTORY

page 123

INDEX

page 125

Today, the game of basketball can fill an arena like the Indiana Hoosier Dome with a crowd the size of a modest city.

Courtesy of Indiana Basketball Hall of Fame

**M**arion is a fairly typical Indiana town, a blue-collar community some sixty miles (96 km) northeast of Indianapolis where Fisher Body and RCA Television plants dominate the physical and economic landscape. On Friday and Saturday nights, each of the 7,500 seats is filled in the high school gym. The Marion Giants, you see, are the only game in this town! "It started in the 1920s," says Bill Green, who once coached at Marion. "It's a farm area here, very flat, and in the winter, it's very cold because there's noth-ing to stop the wind. So people went to the local gym for something to do. As time went on, the com-munities got interested in

Bill Green has coached his high school teams to six Indiana state basketball championships. No other man can say that.

**Jay Edwards of the Marion Giants, left, works against Damon Bailey of Bedford-North Lawrence.**

high school basketball.

"I've got to tell you, it's a way of life here, even today. Actually, it's almost a religion, an obsession with people. Erma's is the only steakhouse in town, and there's two movie theaters at the mall. That's about it. After a while, it became a prestigious thing to see the Marion Giants play. I mean, sixteen-year-old kids become celebrities."

Such basketball fever is common in other Indiana towns as well. Perhaps only Texas high school football fans come close to matching this passion for basketball. Marion sold 6,800 season tickets in 1990, and according to Green, the school

Courtesy of Indiana Basketball Hall of Fame

could have moved twice that in the community of 35,000. Two hundred seats were set aside for the visiting team and another five hundred were reserved for general admission.

Bill Green is best known as the coach of the Marion team that won three consecutive state titles in 1985, 1986, and 1987. It had been done only once before, at Franklin High School, in 1920, 1921, and 1922. In basketball-mad Indiana, Green's feat was as celebrated as discovering the cure for polio. That is because Indiana is one of three remaining states in the nation that have an open-class state high school basketball tournament, which means that all 385 high schools compete in one division. In sectional play, teams are eliminated until there are sixty-four remaining, then thirty-two, and then the Sweet Sixteen. Eventually, one team emerges as the winner. Over a three-year period under Green, Marion went a heart-stopping 86–4, winning forty straight games at one point, the second-longest streak in state history. Green, who earlier won two titles at Marion in 1975 and 1976, and another at Indianapolis' Washington High School with George McGinnis (who would later become a professional player), has coached six state champions, the most in Indiana history.

Even so, "I worked on a one-year contract," Green says. "You've got three-hundred-seventy-odd coaches, and every season you know that about eighty will get fired. The average life span is about four years. That's how intense it gets."

In addition to McGinnis, Green coached a number of players that went on to play college ball at places like Indiana University, North Carolina, and Notre Dame. Today, he coaches at the University of Indianapolis, a Division II college program. He still remembers, however, the electric atmosphere of the Indiana championship games played in Hinkle Field House in Indianapolis. In 1928, when it was called Butler Field House, John Wooden played in the building's debut as the site for the state championship game. Wooden's team, Martinsville, lost 13–12 to Muncie, but he went on to play at Purdue and then to coach at UCLA.

The high school state championship moved first to Indiana University, then to Market Square Arena before finally shifting to the hulking Hoosier Dome in 1990. A record crowd of more than 41,000 watched Damon Bailey's Bedford-North Lawrence team defeat Concord 63–60, but some folks in Indiana seem to have liked it better at Hinkle.

"It was louder and the games seemed more competitive," Green says. "The sound was incredible. There was nothing like a game there to get your heart beating."

Hinkle was where the movie *Hoosiers* was shot in 1986. Set in the 1950s, it follows the improbable success of Hickory High School and its six-boy team through the state tournament all the way to a victory in the finals.

"The idea in Indiana is that every team gets to compete. Theoretically every team has a chance to win the state championship," says Ron Newlin, curator of the Indiana Basketball Hall of Fame. "Now, a Hickory isn't going to win, but there's always the chance of a few upsets in the sectionals. You walk into a four-thousand-seat gym where folks from six different communities are trying to get standing-room tickets, and it all comes back. You don't have to have a kid on the team to get excited about it. For three-and-one-half weeks, time sort of stands still."

If you want to experience it yourself without waiting in line for those standing-room tickets, Newlin's Hall of Fame museum in New Castle, Indiana, thirty-five miles (56 km) east of Indianapolis brings it all home. Sit in the Hall of Fame theater and let the eleven-projector multimedia show take you inside a town at sectionals time.

Larry Joe Bird is just one product of Indiana's basketball fervor. The Boston Celtics star was born in French Lick, Indiana (population 2,265), and played at Springs Valley High School, briefly at Indiana University, and later, at Indiana State before becoming a national treasure who has helped elevate the game to a new height.

# AMERICA'S GAME

From the heartland to the big city, basketball is uniquely America's game. It is a pure and simple sport. No leather gloves are necessary, no hulking shoulder pads or cumbersome equipment. Only a ball and hoop are needed.

And with that equipment, the sweet swishes, bounce passes, and tenacious rebounds have been happening for one hundred years. That's right, in December 1991, basketball celebrated its centennial. In 1891, Dr. James Naismith had a pair of peach baskets nailed to the gymnasium railing at the

*Courtesy of Indiana Basketball Hall of Fame*

School for Christian Workers in Springfield, Massachusetts, to provide exercise and diversion for eighteen of the school's YMCA students. A year later, the *New York Times* wrote an article on Naismith's intriguing game of basket ball (two words then) and the sport began to spread across the country.

Officially soccer is the most viewed sport in the world, but there is evidence that more people in more countries are dribbling on a ninety-four-by-fifty-foot (28.7-by-15.2-m) court with their hands than on a field with their feet. In recent years, basketball has become the world's leading participatory sport. And today, basketball is a global enterprise.

"Increasingly, when you look and see what's happening, whether it's Sony buying a network or somebody buying Rockefeller Center, it's happening in every phase of business and everyday life," says David Stern, the National Basketball Association's (NBA's) commissioner. "Essentially, we are the last global sport to internationalize."

Last, but hardly least. Basketball did not become an Olympic sport until 1936, but today, the sport's international lines are hopelessly blurred. The NBA's 1990–91 regular season opened in Tokyo, Japan, where capacity crowds of 10,111 watched the Phoenix Suns and Utah Jazz split a pair of games. While they didn't always understand the subtleties of the pick-and-roll or illegal defenses, overall the fans were enthusiastic. They were especially fascinated by seven-foot-four (224-cm) Utah center Mark Eaton and Phoenix's six-foot-ten (208-cm)

**The Indiana Basketball Hall of Fame brings you back to the 1950s, when high school basketball was all that mattered to a small town.**

© Ken Levine/Allsport

**Vlade Divac seemed to make the transition from Yugoslavia's national team to the Los Angeles Lakers with ease.**

Saronas, and Alexander. For these players, the real discoveries in North America were things like Pizza Hut, Jeeps, and ESPN. But they could play a bit of basketball as well!

Vlade Divac, whose wedding was televised on national television in Yugoslavia, quietly slipped into a complementary role with the Los Angeles Lakers. Playing less than twenty minutes per game in the 1989–90 season, the seven-foot-one (216-cm) center averaged 8.5 points and 6.4 rebounds. "It is too much. Very, very nice," Divac said of Los Angeles. (And that was before he bought a Porsche.) Saronas Marciulionis, a Soviet guard, signed a three-year deal with the Golden State Warriors worth nearly $4 million, averaged 12.1 points per game, and shot 51.9 percent from the field. He averaged more than twenty-two minutes per game as the Warriors' third guard. "In the Soviet Union," Marciulionis said, "we don't pay attention to rebounding and defense. But here, it's important." Fellow Soviet Alexander Volkov (Atlanta Hawks) and Yugoslavians Zarko Paspalj (San Antonio) and Drazen Petrovic (Portland Trail Blazers) had a bit more difficulty adjusting to the American game.

At the same time, Americans like Danny Ferry and Brian Shaw grappled with the language and social obstacles in a foreign country. Not long ago, prominent college players used the threat of playing in places like Greece or Spain as contract leverage. Now, they really do it. Both Ferry and Shaw played the 1989–90 season in Italy before returning home in 1990. Long-time NBA regulars Earl Cureton and Darryl Dawkins now toil in Italy; former college wizards Milt Wagner (Louisville) and Ken Barlow (Notre Dame) are in Israel; Dallas Comegys and George Gervin play in Spain; Walt Frazier, Jr., is in Cyprus; and Gerald Paddio performs in France. And you are just as likely to find experienced foreigners on America's better college teams. Nadav Henefeld, an Israeli soldier, helped push the University of Connecticut basketball team into the national headlines before returning to play professional ball in Israel. Australian Andrew Gaze similarly lifted the quality of basketball at Seton Hall University.

Stern sees greater things ahead for basketball in the world showcase. "We're mindful of what a great show the World Cup is on a global basis," he says. "We think that over the next decade you're going to see that the world championship of basketball is going to begin to develop similarly."

Tom Chambers. The NBA is the first major American professional sports league to play regular-season games outside of North America. This was the first of what is likely to become a series of marketing experiments in Japan, where investors are already financing the construction of new arenas in Phoenix and Salt Lake City.

## NEW KIDS OFF THE BLOC

With the participation of NBA teams in the international tournament known as the McDonald's Open (the New York Knicks won the 1990 title in Barcelona) and new rules that will allow NBA players to play on Olympic teams, the international trade balance now applies to basketball. In 1989, five of Eastern Europe's best players joined the NBA with varying degrees of success. Jerry Colangelo of the Phoenix Suns saw the emigration coming, and in 1985, he signed Bulgarian forward Georgi Glouchkov to a contract. Glouchkov's inability to keep pace in the NBA reinforced the notion that Eastern Europeans were too rigid and mechanical to flourish in the run-and-gun NBA. That was before the arrival of Vlade, Zarko, Drazen,

# A BIG-TIME, SMALL-SCREEN SUCCESS

In America, people are beginning to pay more attention, too. In the early 1980s, the NBA was not exactly a hot commodity. A majority of teams were losing money, the league's marketing and promotional efforts were nearly invisible, and there was the pervasive view that NBA games were just a lot of running around, devoid of defense or strategy. There was one season when CBS Sports televised only five games. In 1980 and 1981, the network actually showed the league's championship series on tape-delay because it was afraid of a prime-time ratings disaster. In 1983, Ted Shaker became the executive producer of NBA telecasts for CBS Sports. David Stern ascended the NBA throne a year later. It is not a coincidence that this is when the league began to turn around.

"I had seen our telecasts," Shaker says. "I thought there were things we could do better. The sport was sick, but underneath it was a great, great American game. Deep down, I was convinced if it was presented right it could succeed on television."

Previously, the league had been offered in regional markets in an attempt to play on geographical loyalties. Shaker decided to market the NBA nationally as a league of superstars. The Los Angeles Lakers with "Magic" Johnson and the Boston Celtics with Larry Bird became the featured teams. CBS made an effort to find attractive dates to showcase the games and explained the complexities of the game better than it had previously. Meanwhile, Stern tended to the league's financial health. The NBA adopted a salary cap and a revenue-sharing plan that guaranteed that at least 53 percent of the league's gross income would wind up in the hands of players. A powerful drug policy helped remove the image of an undisciplined league.

Ratings improved. Attendance grew. And salaries went through the roof. In 1990, the Cleveland Cavaliers actually signed six-foot-eleven (211-cm) forward John "Hot Rod" Williams, who averaged 13.5 points off the bench the year before, to a seven-year contract worth a staggering $26.5 million. "You are not going to hear me lament that player salaries are going up, because that means revenues are going up," Stern says. "That's the deal we made with the players' association." Blame the Miami Heat. The expansion team, hoping to gener-

ate some interest, tendered Williams that monstrous offer, and the Cavaliers felt compelled to match it. Williams made $60,975 per game in 1990–91, nearly twice the $33,950 Oakland A's slugger Jose Canseco commands from his annual take of $5.5 million. In the wake of the Miami offer and the Cleveland deal, the rest of the NBA is paying the price.

It all comes down to supply and demand. The NBA is, as stars like Magic Johnson and Isiah Thomas and celebrities like Jack Nicholson said in promotional messages, FAN-tastic. Consider the attendance numbers: In 1982–83, the league drew 9,637,614 fans, for an average of 10,220 per game. Attendance has increased every year since. The 1989–90 total was a staggering 17,368,659, an average of 15,690 per game. In 1992–93, attendance again reached record levels, as 17,778,295 fans attended 1,107 games.

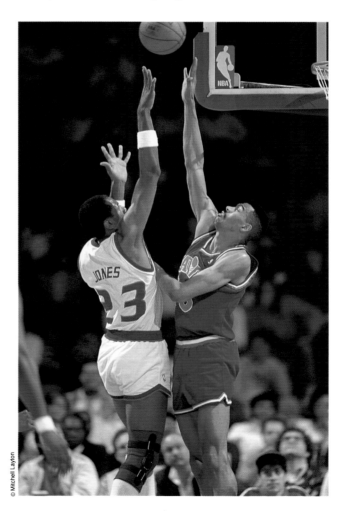

© Mitchell Layton

**John "Hot Rod" Williams is a sound player, but was he worth $26.5 million? For some reason, the Cleveland Cavaliers thought so.**

In 1990, CBS Sports spent more than a billion dollars to gain exclusive control of major league baseball telecasts. NBC Sports countered with a $600 million offer for the four-year rights to the NBA. Previously, CBS had paid $173 million for a similar package. And so, the league rolls on. Although television ratings for sports have declined in the last decade, basketball, both professional and college, has done remarkably well. Expansion franchises in Miami, Minneapolis, Charlotte, and Orlando have diluted the quality of play, but the games are often still riveting.

The college game has also grown immensely. In 1939, an eight-team field, including Brown University and Utah State, was assembled, and Oregon defeated Ohio State, 46–33, to win the first formal National Collegiate Athletic Association (NCAA) men's basketball championship. Total attendance for the tournament was 15,025. More than fifty years later, sixty-four teams are seeded in the tournament and attendance has climbed past 600,000. There was a time when only a handful of teams had a chance to win the national title. Between 1964 and 1973, UCLA won nine of ten championships under coach John Wooden, including seven straight. In the 1980s, only Indiana and Louisville, won more than a single title. In the 1990s, there are at least twenty teams each season that have the potential to win the national championship.

# THE GREATEST OF EASE

The play is the thing. . . . And the stars. There is Jordan, the six-foot-six (198-cm), 198-pound (89.8-kg) guard for the Chicago Bulls. He is breathtaking on the court. Jordan won an amazing seven straight scoring titles from 1986–87 through 1992–93, tying Wilt Chamberlain's all-time NBA record. There is David Robinson, the former Navy lieutenant, who rocketed onto the scene in 1989–90 after serving two years in the military. He helped the San Antonio Spurs to improve thirty-five games in a single season, to 56–26 and to a berth in the Western Conference semifinals. Robinson averaged 24.3 points and twelve rebounds per game. New York Knicks center Patrick Ewing still operates at giddy levels of efficiency, and there are talented younger players behind him: Houston Rockets center Hakeem Olajuwon, Phoenix Suns forward Charles Barkley, Phoenix Suns guard Kevin Johnson, Utah Jazz guard John Stockton, and Utah player Karl Malone.

Their athleticism, at times, defies description. You will not find such superbly conditioned athletes in any other major professional sport. Hockey players glide on skates and only play a few minutes at a time. There would be no place for the Chicago Bears' rotund William "The Refrigerator" Perry in the NBA, who, at six foot one (185 cm), weighs more than 330 pounds (150 kg). Barkley, once known as the "Round Mound of Rebound" is six foot six (198 cm) and weighs a relatively svelte 252 pounds (114 kg)—all muscle and gristle. And Perry probably couldn't run up and down the court for a twelve-minute quarter, let alone for a full forty-eight-minute game. Match virtually any basketball player against a baseball player in a half-mile race and the basketball player is likely to win every time. While baseball players run ninety feet (27.4 m) at a time, four or five times a game, basketball players continually run the length of the ninety-four-foot (28.7-m) court during a game. And, since there are only ten players on the floor at a time and each one's participation is continuous, basketball players exert far more individually than those in baseball or football, where there are eighteen and twenty-two athletes playing simultaneously and the individual's performance is not as constant.

Dr. Naismith probably never imagined the spectacle of Julius Erving in full flight or the grace of seven-foot-two (218-cm) Kareem Abdul-Jabbar dropping his Skyhook into the net. Or the intensity of a high school game in Marion, Indiana. Or the bouncing of basketballs in China.

In 1936, Naismith attended the Olympic Games in Berlin, Germany, where basketball was an official sport for the first time. "As I talked to those superb athletes from all quarters of the globe," he wrote, "I realized that the game I had invented back in Springfield, Massachusetts, had had a fine part in the development of better international understanding.

"Collectors of statistics say that some ninety million admissions were paid to see the youth of the nation perform on basketball courts last year. The game of basketball has made quite an advance in interest since the day when a small group of young men first tossed a ball into a couple of peach baskets nailed to a gymnasium railing."

© Tim DeFrisco/Allsport

Anyone can throw a ball through a hoop, but the world-class athletes are what make today's game of basketball so breathtaking. Here, Michael Jordan of the Chicago Bulls floats like a butterfly and stings like a bee.

When drop-the-handkerchief wasn't enough to keep his students occupied during the long New England winter, Dr. James Naismith came up with a new game involving peach baskets and a soccer ball.

## CHAPTER ONE

# THE EVOLUTION OF BASKETBALL

I n December 1881, before the era of Julius Erving and sophisticated zone defenses, Dr. James Naismith was faced with a dilemma. This instructor at the School for Christian Workers in Springfield, Massachusetts, had eighteen restless students on his hands and needed an outlet for their energy. Pressure increased when Dr. Luther Gulick, the school's president, repeatedly brought up the issue in faculty meetings. "No problems arose so long as we could get out of doors for exercise," Naismith wrote later, "but when winter came, my worries began. Those boys simply would not play drop-the-hand-kerchief!" It was then that Naismith directed the jani-

Nearly a century after Naismith sketched out the first rules for basketball, players like Julius Erving were flying through the air with the greatest of ease.

**This unremarkable four-story building on the corner of State and Sherman Streets in Springfield, Massachusetts, was the site of the first basketball game in December 1891. A shopping center would eventually replace it.**

tor to attach boxes to the railings at opposite ends of the school's sixty-five-by-forty-five-foot (19.8-by-13.7-m) gymnasium. The janitor used peach baskets, which he nailed to each railing, ten feet (3 m) above the gym floor. Naismith appropriated the positions from the Canadian game of lacrosse and instructed the nine players on each side to shoot a soccer ball at the goals. Here are the highlights of Naismith's original thirteen rules that he posted on the gym door:

1) The ball may be thrown in any direction with one or two hands.

2) The ball may be batted in any direction with one or both hands, but never the fist.

3) A player cannot run with the ball.

4) The ball must be held in or between the hands.

5) No shouldering, holding, pushing, tripping, or striking in any way the person of an opponent shall be allowed; the first infringement of this rule by any player should count as a foul; the second shall disqualify him until the next goal is made.

6) A goal shall be made when the ball is thrown or batted from the ground into the basket and stays there, providing those defending the goal do not touch or disturb the goal.

7) When the ball goes out of bounds, it shall be thrown onto the field of play by the first person touching it. In case of a dispute, the umpire shall throw it straight onto the field. The thrower-in is allowed five seconds; if he holds it any longer, it shall go to the opponent.

8) The time shall be two fifteen-minute halves, with five minutes of rest between.

9) The side making the most goals in that time shall be declared the winner. In the case of a draw, the game may, by

agreement of the captains, be continued until another goal is made.

It was a stroke of genius. The game could be played indoors during the winter when baseball and football fields were frozen and under snow. It was a fast-moving, exciting game and solved the exercise problem at the YMCA school. A month later, the school magazine described the game, and two months later, the first public game was staged between students and teachers. Before a crowd of two hundred, the students handled the teachers, five goals to one. Amos Alonzo Stagg, who would later become famous as a football coach, scored the teachers' only goal. In April 1892, the *New York Times* wrote a story about this new game developed in the gyms of Springfield. Details of the game passed through the YMCA network, and by the end of the year, basketball was being played in distant places like Pennsylvania and Iowa. Naismith later brought the game to Denver and the University of Kansas. The man who once studied to be a minister had created a different religion altogether. Naismith had the good fortune to see his game sweep the world.

"Basketball coaches have become more proficient, some developing man-to-man defense and others the zone system," Naismith wrote in 1939 (the last of his seventy-eight years). "The more I watch the game, the more I realize that while easy to understand and simple to demonstrate, it is nevertheless a challenge to skill. It is only through grounding in the fundamentals and constant practice that championships are won. This challenge to perfection in execution of the plays is, to my mind, one of the attractions of the game for the pure pleasure it brings to the players. Just how many persons engage in the game of basketball, no one knows, but the number must be large."

The number is even larger and the game more sophisticated today. In many ways, the game hasn't changed much; the goal is still to drop a twelve-inch (30-cm) ball through an eighteen-inch (46-cm) basket. But there have been some refinements. A year after the peach baskets were first hung, they were replaced by cylindrical baskets made of heavy woven wire. Backboards arrived in 1893. Regulation balls were created in 1894, the same year free throws were introduced and the free-throw line crept in from twenty feet (6.1 m) to the present-day fifteen feet (4.6 m). In 1895, the value of a goal

was changed from three points to two, and free throws were reduced from three points to one. Two years later, five-man teams became the norm. For the next fifty-seven years, basketball remained essentially unchanged, with the exceptions that in 1932 the three-second rule was added to prevent players from camping out under the basket, in 1937 the center jump after each goal was eliminated, and in 1952, the foul lane was widened from six to twelve feet (from 1.8 to 3.7 m).

On October 30, 1954, a new rule changed the game profoundly. In an attempt to end stalling, the executives of the NBA introduced the twenty-four-second clock at the urging of Syracuse owner Danny Biasone. He used some elementary math to figure the typical number of shots per minute in an NBA game—about 120 shots came to 2.5 for each of the game's forty-eight minutes. That worked out to one every twenty-four seconds. The complementary rule required teams to shoot at the opponent's basket within the twenty-four seconds, which demanded a faster-paced game and radically altered strategy. Now, pushing the ball up the court quickly became important.

During the 1953–54 season, each team went from averaging sixty shots per game to between seventy-five and eighty. As the tempo increased, so did spectator interest in the game. The fast-break game, the trademark of the Boston Celtics in the 1960s, was as compelling to watch as it was successful. Without the twenty-four-second clock, Wilt Chamberlain probably wouldn't have scored 100 points during a single game in 1962. Most basketball officials accredit the twenty-four-second clock with saving the NBA from extinction.

Initially, the game was intended to favor people standing six feet (183 cm) tall, and most rule changes were directed at diminishing this advantage. The three-second rule encouraged big men to become more agile. The twenty-four-second clock placed more of a premium on speed and quickness; it also prevented taller teams from holding onto the ball when they got ahead late in the game.

In 1967, college officials outlawed the slam dunk. This went over about as well as Prohibition nearly a half-century earlier. Ten years later, it was back. In June 1979, NBA owners chose to de-emphasize big men again by voting 15–7 to experiment with the three-point shot. Critics argued that the American Basketball Association (ABA) had tried it, and it had folded.

"Larry Legend," as they call Larry Joe Bird in Boston, was the complete basketball player the wide-open modern game demands.

Changing the two-point basket, some argued, was immoral. Still, NBA players who shot successfully from outside the twenty-two-foot (6.7-m) line at the corners (twenty-three feet and nine inches [7.2 m] at the center of the floor) were rewarded with three points. Fred "Downtown" Brown of Seattle was the first league champion, sinking thirty-nine of eighty-eight, for a percentage of 44.3 in 1979–80. The colleges, led by Ed Steitz, soon followed suit and adopted the three-point rule, although the line was drawn some three feet (.9 m) closer to the basket. Steitz also helped introduce the forty-five-second clock to colleges in 1985.

The result of these modifications is a wide-open game that demands agility and athleticism. And with all the rule changes over the years, there is still room for the six-footer (183–cm) for whom Naismith originally created the game.

## THE BASICS

After several weeks of listening to his children whine, the father grudgingly bought a six-by-six-foot (1.8-by-1.8-m) piece of plywood. The boys painted it white, and the father bolted it into the side of the red barn that served as the family garage. As it turned out, the rim they attached, was about six inches (15 cm) too high. The cinder driveway didn't always offer the truest bounces, but it was an adequate court on which to practice the fundamentals of basketball. Their shots weren't always accurate, but that just meant more rebounds to go after; their passing was not exactly artistic, but their free-throw shooting did approach mediocre. Slam dunks didn't happen . . . yet. But that's what dreams are for. And that's how many of today's best players began.

## The Shot

This is as basic as it gets in basketball. The object: Put the ball in the hole. Few did it better than Los Angeles Lakers guard Jerry West. Only three men, Michael Jordan, Wilt Chamberlain, and Elgin Baylor, produced a better scoring average in NBA history than West's 27.0 over fourteen seasons. He had one of the prettiest shots ever.

© R. Mackson/FPG International

Speaking about the shot, West, now the Lakers' general manager, says: "First, you've got to know when and from where to shoot. Second, you have to know how to get room and time for your shot, as well as what type of shot to attempt. Finally, you've got to use the correct mechanical technique or all you'll do is give somebody a chance to get a rebound. No one can be a sixty-percent shooter all over the court, but you develop spots where you're seventy-five or eighty percent. The ball should be held with the fingertips of the shooting hand, just far enough back in the hand to be felt lightly with the palm. Cradle it in the V formed by the thumb and index finger. The elbow must be kept fairly close to the body and directly under the hand through the entire shot. The off hand guides the ball, and the lift comes from the legs in a smooth sweep, followed by a downward, slightly inward snap of the wrist and a good extension of the hand and arm."

Easy, right? As a guard, West's shots came from the perimeter, the fifteen-to-eighteen-foot (4.6-to-5.5-m) range, or on drives to the basket. (Forwards shoot from the corners or closer to the basket, while centers begin most shot sequences with their backs to the basket before powering closer.) In the game's early days, players used two hands because the ball seemed easier to manage that way. And then Angelo "Hank" Luisetti of Stanford University revolutionized the two-handed set shot just before World War II with a daring one-hand shot. It wasn't long before players took Luisetti's shot and transformed it into a one-hand jump shot that could be delivered in almost no time.

## The Rebound

If the very best shooters make about half of their shots, it follows that for every successful shot there is a clunker, a

**Karl Malone of the Utah Jazz, one of the game's eminent power forwards, must rebound as well as score.**

rebound for the taking. Technically, scoring determines the game's outcome, but rebounding is just as important. "Every rebound a team gets is worth, I figure, up to six points," says Chamberlain. "Most games are won and lost by fewer points than that, so if you have to risk a few bumps and bruises going after a missed shot, I say it's worth it. If a shot hits, it's two points. If a shot misses, the offense has the chance to get the ball back so it can work for another attempt. The difference between three points one way [with a foul] and the other is six points."

Chamberlain knows quite a little bit about rebounding. He heads the NBA's all-time list with 23,924, followed by arch-rival Bill Russell (21,620) and Kareem Abdul-Jabbar (17,440). Chamberlain led the league in rebounding an astounding eleven times. Obviously, being tall helps. Consider Chamberlain at seven foot one (216 cm), Russell at six foot ten (208 cm), and Abdul-Jabbar at seven foot two (218 cm). And Moses Malone, who is six foot ten (208 cm), led the NBA in rebounding six times, two more than Russell. His specialty was rebounds at the offensive end. On February 9, 1979, he grabbed thirty-seven rebounds against New Orleans.

"Height and good jumping ability are advantages in offensive rebounding, but they are by no means the only factors in becoming a good rebounder," Malone says. "There are some instances during the course of the NBA season when a seven-foot (213-cm) center is outbattled for a rebound, even by a player as much as six inches (15 cm) shorter. Rebounding is a skill improved by these three ingredients: aggressiveness, positioning, and determination. A good way to get out of the habit of watching shots before going in for the rebound is to automatically think that every shot taken will be missed. This will force you to anticipate where you think the shot will come off the rim."

Says Portland Trail Blazers power forward Buck Williams, who reached the 1,000-rebound mark in five different seasons, "My rebounding motto is 'The ball belongs to me.' Rebounding on the offensive board is something that I've taken pride in throughout my career. It takes a lot of hard work to be good at rebounding, but there's nothing more satisfying than a good rebound pulled down in a crowd under the glass, and then going back up with it, scoring, and getting a foul shot, too."

Height, as the Atlanta Hawks' Moses Malone demonstrates here, is not always as important as heart for rebounding. Malone, giving some eight inches, beat seven-foot-six Manute Bol to this ball.

Next page: New York Knicks' center Patrick Ewing is a throwback to the days of Russell and Chamberlain, the two players who dominated the game both on offense and defense as no one before or since.

## The Assist

The no-look pass or the behind-the-back pass can send a crowd into hysterics, but an effective chest or bounce pass to the open man is what generally leads to an easy shot. The *assist*, the pass that sets up a successful basket, is an art in itself, and Oscar Robertson was a master. Robertson led all NBA players with 9,887 assists until 1990–91, when his record was surpassed by Magic Johnson who is now the all-time leader with 9,921. This Los Angeles Lakers point guard is six foot nine (206 cm) and has an amazing court presence. Johnson led the league in assists in 1982–83, 1983–84, 1985–86, and 1986–87, and holds the record for most playoff assists as well.

"Passing the basketball is the quickest and most effective way to get the ball from player to player and move it around the court," Johnson says. "The more passes that are made by the offense, the more you will challenge the defense and keep

them scrambling, frustrated, and tired. The perfect end result of a series of well-executed passes will be a pass made to an open player close to the basket who just takes the ball and scores easily. It's not shooting that will win the game for you, it's the passing that went into setting up those winning shots. I love to pass. It gives me a thrill to have the ball end up in the hands of the right player who's just ready to put it in the bucket for two points. A pass, no matter how difficult or simple it is to make, is only good if it can be caught by your teammate. You can't overpower the ball or your teammate

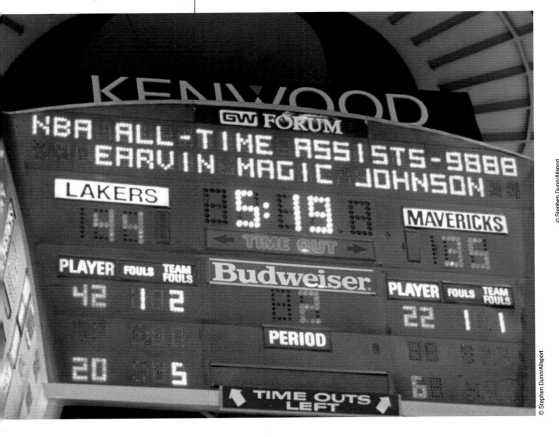

# THE BASKETBALL HALL OF FAME

Walk into the Naismith Memorial Basketball Hall of Fame in Springfield, Massachusetts, and the unmistakable sound of basketballs bouncing off iron rims drifts into the lobby. No, it isn't ghosts of yesterday, and it's not Rick Barry working on his free throws. Visitors are encouraged to step up to the "Shoot-Out!" display, where they can throw shots from different distances. And there is also the "How High Is Up?" exhibit, where would-be Dr. J's can test their vertical leaping ability.

The Honors Court is where all the basketball greats enshrined since 1959 can be found. Dr. James Naismith himself is there, as is Wilt Chamberlain. They are all there,

studies in bronze, preserved for posterity. And there is more: You can follow the game's development at all levels, from high school to college to the professionals. There are high school uniforms and pictures of players like Kareem Abdul-Jabbar, Bob Cousy, Cheryl Miller, Bill Bradley, and Patrick Ewing. The college history is treated with reverence here, with documentation of the growth of the NCAA Tournament and the National Invitation Tournament (NIT). The professionals are represented by a display of their uniforms, including some hulking basketball sneakers. And there is a section on the flamboyant and successful college coaches.

Television monitors are everywhere, bringing the game to life. You can see the 1990 NCAA championship games, both men's and women's, and a number of other big games. There are special movies and an international display. The Hall of Fame, once housed at basketball's birthplace, the campus of Springfield College, moved to downtown Springfield in 1985. In its first year there, it drew more than 100,000 visitors from around the world.

**The Basketball Hall of Fame in Springfield, Massachusetts, has a little something for everyone. Balloons, of course, are extra.**

won't be able to hang into it. I try to make my passes soft enough so my man can do something with it right away."

For the record, Bob Cousy of the Boston Celtics was the league's top assist man a record eight times, followed by Robertson (six), and Kevin Porter, who is tied with Johnson with four passing titles. Today, John Stockton is the league's most prolific passer. He has already recorded the four highest totals in history (1,164 in 1990–91, 1,134 in 1989–90, 1,128 in 1987–88, and 1,126 in 1991–92). His best effort in a single game is twenty-seven. During the 1990–91 season, Orlando Magic guard Scott Skiles broke the thirteen-year record of twenty-nine that belonged to Porter. On December 31, 1990, against Denver, Skiles handed out a stunning thirty assists in a 155–116 victory. As a *rookie* for the Milwaukee Bucks in 1986–87, Skiles' total for the season was forty-five.

## The Free Throw

It is a simple thing, the free throw. Nine-year-old kids can toss them in with regularity. Older players, who can no longer glide to the basket, hoist them from the foul line, fifteen feet (4.6 m) from the basket. How hard can this be?

Plenty hard if there are fifteen thousand spectators screaming at you. Awfully hard if the game is hanging in the balance. Terribly hard if the season depends on you making that cupcake of a fifteen-foot shot. All things being equal, and they rarely are, sinking a free throw at the NBA level is mostly a mental enterprise. Most players at that level, Chamberlain aside, can make an open fifteen-foot shot. Why, then, do so many miss from the free-throw line?

"Free throws are all about concentration," says Larry Bird, formerly of the Boston Celtics. "You practice and practice shooting them, and it gets to be second nature. You just have to step up there confident that you're going to make them."

Some players, apparently, would rather have a defensive player in their shorts than face the one-on-one challenge of man versus rim. Take Chamberlain, for example. His lifetime shooting percentage from the line was a sobering 51.1. That means in fourteen seasons he launched 11,862 free throws, made 6,057, and missed 5,805. You can be sure the majority of Chamberlain's shots from the field were from a lot closer than

fifteen feet. Maybe he just couldn't get motivated for a one-point shot.

The free-throw shooters who rate highest in the record book come as no surprise. Rick Barry, Calvin Murphy, Larry Bird, and Bill Sharman have all been diligent players with unnatural levels of concentration. They managed to find a rhythm at the line and block everything else out. Barry is the NBA's all-time leader with a round success rate of 90 percent. He is followed by Murphy (89.2), Bird (88.4), and Sharman (88.3). Sharman led the league seven times, and Barry is a six-time free-throw champion. Murphy has the best single-season mark, an amazing 95.8. In 1980–81, Murphy made 206 of 215 shots from the line. Midway through that season, Murphy made seventy-eight consecutive free throws to set a new NBA record. Nine years later, Bird fell seven free throws short of tying his record. If he had just practiced more. . . .

## The Slam Dunk

Technically, a thundering slam dunk is worth exactly the same as a fluffy, eighteen-foot (5.5-m) jump shot launched from the perimeter—two points. But that's on paper. The slam dunk is the highest percentage shot there is, because when you ram the ball through the iron hoop, little is left to chance. The slam can have a powerful effect on a game; the dunkee and the partisan crowd are stirred by a sensational slam, while the opponent becomes disheartened.

Dominique Wilkins, the Atlanta Hawks forward, has refined the art of dunking to a science. "Although the shot is spectacular and appears to be unrehearsed, it actually isn't," Wilkins says. "Your practice sessions and scrimmages are the time to be creative with the different dunks. This way you will have a good idea of what you can and cannot do in an actual game situation."

Once every game or two, a dunk is missed because the player misjudged the target or encountered interference on the way to the basket. Most of the time, however, the ball hits its mark. Wilkins is six foot nine (206 cm), but his leaping ability allows him to slam-dunk with ease. Usually, it is the taller players who slam. Artis Gilmore, for instance, stood seven foot two (218 cm), and over a career that spanned

© Tim DeFrisco/Allsport

**David Robinson of the San Antonio Spurs is the best and the brightest of the young slam-dunk breed.**

twelve seasons, he produced a shooting percentage of .599, the best in NBA history. And you can bet he wasn't firing away from three-point country. Many of Gilmore's shots were stuffs in close. Wilt Chamberlain, "the Big Dipper," posted three of the five best shooting seasons in history, including a staggering 72.7 percent in 1972–73, when he made 426 of 586 shots, including countless slams. The other two top-five performances were Gilmore's.

So devastating and malicious was the slam dunk that in 1967 the NCAA banned it in competition. UCLA coach John Wooden maintained that the rule was aimed at his slam-dunking star Lew Alcindor (later Kareem Abdul-Jabbar). Still, he admitted that the rule made his towering center a more complete player because it forced him to develop a variety of soft shots around the basket and a turnaround jump shot. In 1976, the NCAA came to its senses. After a ten-year hiatus, the most exciting play in basketball was returned to the college game.

## THE CULT HEROES

In the NBA, where six-foot-five (196-cm) guards and six-foot-ten (208-cm) forwards are the norm, there is something endearing and enduring about a man who stands seven foot seven (231 cm). Or, perhaps, one who is five foot three (160 cm). That is the long and short of it these days in the NBA. By coincidence, Manute Bol (the long) and Tyrone "Mug-

**In a world dominated by big guys, how can you resist the little guys? Tyrone "Muggsy" Bogues, at five foot three, comes up short of Magic Johnson's chest, but his quicker-than-light speed more than compensates for a lack of height.**

© Ken Levine/Allsport

averaged a career-high 9.4 points per game and had the league's best assist-to-turnover ratio (5.96 to 1).

Still, it is Bogues' sixty-three inches (160 cm) that leaves people thinking of him as a novelty act. Everywhere he goes, people are drawn to him. "It's like that all the time in airports," says Bogues' Charlotte teammate Armon Gilliam. "We don't have a lot of big names on our team, but everyone knows Muggsy. He's small and recognizable. He's our mascot."

Bol, the tallest player in the history of the league, was born in Gogrial, Sudan, a member of the Dinka Tribe, and grew up playing soccer and handball. Bol wound up playing basketball at Bridgeport University for the 1984–85 season. What a season it was! He towered over the competition, averaging 22.5 points, 13.5 rebounds, and seven blocked shots in thirty-one games. He led the nation with 217 blocked shots. During the summer, he played with the Rhode Island Gulls of the United States Basketball League and established league records for rebounds in a game (28) and blocked shots (18).

While Bol dominated in college play, his weight (225 pounds/102 kg) worked against him in the professional ranks. Extraordinarily thin, Bol was not viewed as an offensive threat. Nevertheless, the Bullets took him in the second round and Bol played in Washington for three seasons. He blocked fifteen shots in a 1986 game against Atlanta and did it again against Indiana in 1987. His 397 blocked shots as a rookie were the second-highest total in league history. Bol was traded to the Golden State Warriors in 1988 and then to the Philadelphia 76ers in 1990, where he continued to be a presence on defense.

There are other NBA curiosities. Anthony Jerome "Spud" Webb stands five foot seven (170 cm) and regularly excites Atlanta Hawks fans. Webb averaged a creditable 6.7 points and 4.5 assists per game in his first five professional seasons. Utah center Mark Eaton stands seven foot four (223 cm) and has blocked 2,592 shots, second on the all-time list behind Kareem Abdul-Jabbar. Chuck Nevitt, at seven foot five (226 cm), was the second-tallest player in the NBA. He weighs only 225 pounds (102 kg) and has a thirty-eight-inch (96-cm) waist, remarkable for someone of his height. Nevitt was originally a third-round draft choice of the Houston Rockets but has also spent time with the Milwaukee Bucks, the Los Angeles Lakers, the San Antonio Spurs, and the Detroit Pistons.

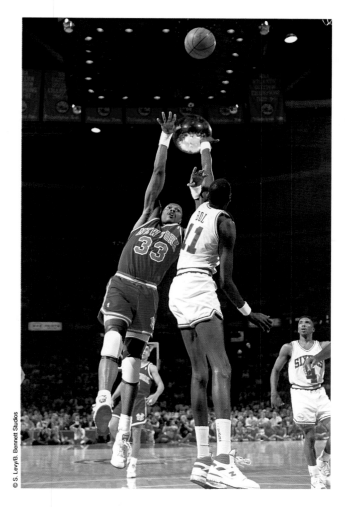

gsy" Bogues (the short) are listed consecutively in the NBA register. They also played together in 1987–88 for the Washington Bullets.

Bol and Bogues are two of the league's cult heroes, but this doesn't mean they can't play, too. Take Bogues, for example. Despite his (lack of) size, Bogues was the twelfth overall pick in the 1987 draft by the Bullets, after a strong career at Wake Forest University. Bogues was less of a scorer (8.3 points per game) than an offensive catalyst. He is unnaturally quick and his size allows him to maneuver around most of the tall players on the court. Passing and court vision are his greatest gifts. In his third season, 1989–90, Bogues produced 867 assists for the Charlotte Hornets, putting him fourth in the league with an average of 10.7. (The first three were John Stockton, Magic Johnson, and Kevin Johnson.) Bogues also

**The frightening thing about Manute Bol is that he doesn't have to leave his feet to block a shot, as Patrick Ewing will testify.**

**Next page: The success of Anthony "Spud" Webb proves that there is always room for the little man in basketball.**

He averages about five minutes and two points per game, but they love him in Houston, where he is known as the Human Victory Cigar. When he enters the game, it's usually over. "I still dream about being a star someday, but what the hey," Nevitt says. "I can at least say that I dunked on Bill Cartwright and once blocked a shot by Dr. J." Philadelphia's 1993 first-round draft choice, Shawn Bradley from Brigham Young University, is a statuesque seven foot six.

And then there is Kurt Rambis. For reasons even he can't explain, the six-foot-eight (203-cm) journeyman forward has inspired a cult following that has stretched all the way to Japan. When he played for the Lakers, some young fans took to wearing his trademark black glasses and false mustaches. They called themselves the Rambis Youth. When the Phoenix Suns played the Utah Jazz in Japan in late 1990, several Japanese fans were spotted in black glasses and mustaches. It was another mysterious appearance by the Rambis Youth.

## BASKETBALL IN THE OLYMPICS

There was a time when basketball was dominated solely by the United States. Between 1936, when basketball was first embraced as an Olympic sport, and 1972, the U.S. Olympics basketball team won each of the sixty-three games it played. On September 9, 1972, the streak came to a controversial end. The Soviet team beat the Americans 51–50 to win the gold medal on a disputed call at the end of the game. That was considered an aberration when the U.S. team went another sixteen years without losing. But then the John Thompson–coached team that included David Robinson and Danny Manning managed only the bronze medal in the 1988 Summer Olympics in Seoul, South Korea. As 1992 dawned, however, Olympic basketball again belonged to the United States.

This was because of a 1989 ruling by the international governing body of basketball that permitted professionals to play Olympic basketball beginning with the 1992 Olympic Games in Barcelona, Spain. The "Dream Team," as the team selected for this ground-breaking moment in basketball was called, dominated the sport at the Olympics and helped bring the popularity of basketball to unprecedented levels. The United States team, which consisted of NBA stars Michael Jordan,

© Brian Drake

Larry Bird, Magic Johnson, Karl Malone, Charles Barkley, Patrick Ewing, Scottie Pippen, David Robinson, John Stockton, Chris Mullin, and Clyde Drexler, obliterated the field, beating the Croatian team for the gold medal. Duke's Christian Laettner was the only college player selected for the team, and he played only sparingly. Chuck Daly, the former coach of the two-time NBA champion Detroit Pistons, led a staff of talented coaches culled from the professional and college ranks.

The decisive gold-medal game was held on August 8, 1992. The final score was U.S. 117, Croatia 85; players, spectators, and experts all felt that this was surprisingly close. When individual scores were tallied at game's end, seven Dream Teamers were in double figures: Jordan (22), Barkley (17), Ewing (15), Pippen (12), Johnson and Mullin (both 11), and Drexler (10). The leading scorer for the Croatian team was Drazen Petrovic, the Croatian-born guard for the New Jersey Nets, who had elected to represent his native land in the Olympics; Petrovic died in a tragic car accident in 1993.

# THE HARLEM GLOBETROTTERS

On January 7, 1927, a promoter named Abe Saperstein packed five black basketball players and himself into a Model-T Ford to make the fifty-mile (80-km) journey from Chicago to Hinckley, Illinois. It was the first public appearance of the Harlem Globetrotters and the beginning of a love affair with the public that continues today. Over the years, the Harlem Globetrotters have carried the game of basketball to an international audience. These days, the Globetrotters perform their magic to the tune of "Sweet Georgia Brown" and are seen more as goodwill ambassadors, but at their inception, the games they played were quite real.

Saperstein was born in London on July 4, 1902, and arrived in the United States at the age of six. He grew to the height of only five foot three (160 cm), but played for the bantam basketball team at Chicago's Lake View High School and later played for and coached the Chicago Reds.

Saperstein, a sound businessman, shrewdly packaged a team of black players in hopes of attracting largely white audiences. Although the team was based in Chicago, Saperstein thought *Harlem* evoked romantic images of that pulsating part of New York (remember, this was the 1920s). And the *Globetrotters*? "It sounds," Saperstein reasoned, "as if we've been around."

The Globetrotters were an instant hit and drew enthusiastic and appreciative audiences. On February 3, 1949, the Globetrotters beat the Minneapolis Lakers, the reigning NBA champions. In 1952, they became the first team to complete an around-the-world tour that included London, Europe, North Africa, Bangkok, Singapore, Hong Kong, and the Philippines. In four months, the Globetrotters won 108 games in fifty-eight cities before a combined audience of 1.1 million.

Wilt Chamberlain played for the Globetrotters in 1958–59 before joining the NBA, giving the team further credibility. But over time, the Globetrotters turned more and more toward humor and entertainment. With frontmen like Meadowlark Lemon and Curly Neal, they performed elaborate weaves in front of the basket and a number of scripted gags. In 1985, Lynette Woodward became the first woman to star with the Globetrotters. Their long tradition continues today with two Globetrotter units traveling all over the United States and around the world.

© Brian Drake/Sportschrome East/West

**The search for laughter is always fruitful when the Harlem Globetrotters are in town. The gags are decades old, but they're still funny.**

A forward isn't just a forward anymore. The Atlanta Hawks' Dominique Wilkins (21), for instance, is a finesse forward, while Sir Charles Barkley of the Philadelphia 76ers (34) is a pure power forward. Michael Adams of the Denver Nuggets, opposite, is a guard with both passing and shooting skills.

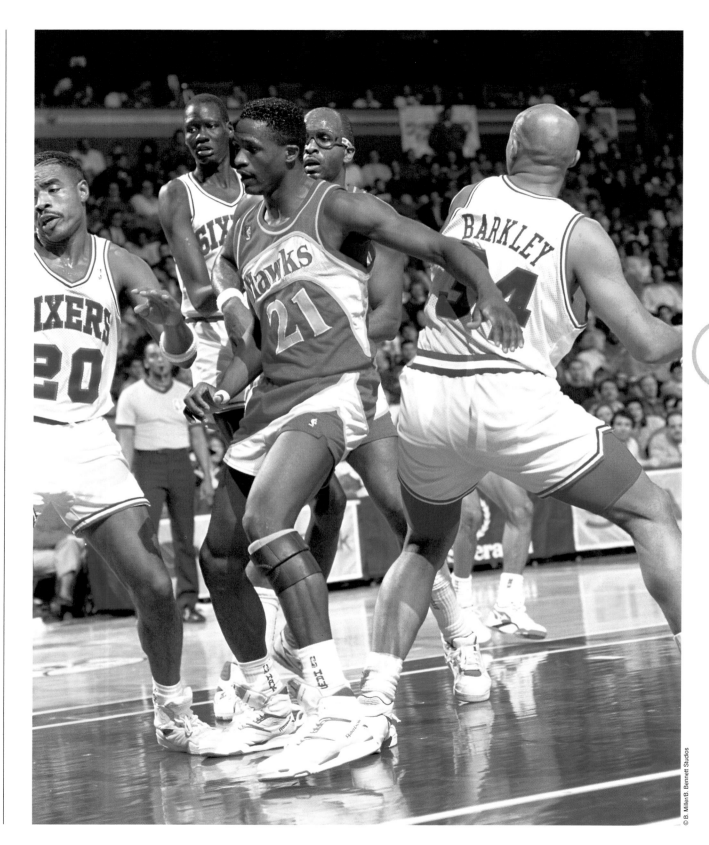

# THE POSITIONS

Broken down into its essential elements, basketball is a by-the-numbers game. The *point guard*, the player who runs the offense and distributes the ball, is referred to as number one. The *shooting guard*, the one who provides instant offense, is number two. The *small* or *finesse forward* is charged primarily with scoring and is known as number three. The *power forward*, num-ber four, is usually a bruis-ing rebounder who is concerned with defense and positioning first, and scoring second. The *center*, the player in the middle, is number five.

# THE POINT GUARD (1)

Calling Earvin "Magic" Johnson a point guard almost missed the point. Johnson, who retired from the Los Angeles Lakers before the 1991–92 season after being diagnosed as HIV positive, had all the tools you look for in a point man: peripheral vision, intelligence, ball-handling skills. He also had an out-of-this-world, six-foot-nine (206-cm), 225-pound (102-kg) body. It wasn't a fair fight.

After the 1989–90 season, at the age of thirty, Johnson was named the Most Valuable Player of the NBA. It was his second consecutive MVP title and his third in four years. Only five other players have ever won the award three times: Kareem Abdul-Jabbar, Bill Russell, Wilt Chamberlain, Moses Malone, and Larry Bird. None of them have ever been point guards.

"Earvin is the smartest man in the league, a true genius in the game," said Pat Riley, who coached Johnson in Los Angeles. "He is taking the game to a new level. He's trying to beat the game itself. The bottom line is we lost the greatest player in history, Kareem Abdul-Jabbar, and we're better."

In the pivot, Johnson was seen as the table-setter for the game's most prolific scorer, Kareem Abdul-Jabbar, the player who lobbed the ball to the big man before he unleashed his lethal Skyhook. When Abdul-Jabbar retired, Johnson exerted himself more as a scorer and rebounder. He even used his Baby Skyhook, learned from the master himself, to produce gritty, inside points. Still, Johnson's greatest gift was controlling the game from the point.

"I had to do different things," Johnson says. "My role changed and it was a challenge. I worked on the three-point shot to give my game more versatility. It made me harder to guard. Without Kareem, I posted up more than I ever had. And I think I became pretty good at that."

"At some point over the years," Riley says, "he has shown his total skill, whether it be offense, passing, defense, or rebounding. But he has always pigeon-holed himself as a top point guard, the delivery man, the run-the-show type, and left the scoring to other people."

Johnson presented an impossible matchup for an opposing defense. He was a half foot (15 cm) taller than many of the point guards he faced, allowing him to shoot over them or forcing teams to put a bigger man on him. That created an-

other problem, since Johnson's quickness gave him a half-step on almost any player his size. This left a teammate, like forward James Worthy, with a terrific height advantage on his defender since teams have only so many big men. Johnson's unique style was based on his ability to get to the basket under almost any circumstance. Only the six-foot-five (196-cm), 220-pound (100-kg) Oscar Robertson systematically destroyed defenses as thoroughly as Johnson.

In Game Six of the celebrated 1980 NBA Championship series, in the absence of injured Abdul-Jabbar, Johnson played center for the first time since high school (only three years prior). Giving nearly three inches (8 cm) and forty pounds (18 kg) to Philadelphia's Darryl Dawkins, the rookie played forty-seven minutes and produced forty-two points, fifteen rebounds, seven assists, three steals, and a blocked shot. Dawkins could only manage fourteen points and four rebounds.

"What position did I play?" Johnson asked himself after the game. "Well, I played center, a little forward, some guard. I tried to think up a name for it, but the best I came up with was center-forward-guard rover."

His enthusiasm is legendary. In the first game of his professional career, the Lakers beat the Clippers at the Los Angeles Sports Arena and Johnson ran across the court to embrace Abdul-Jabbar. "Earvin," said an amused Abdul-Jabbar, "do you realize that we have eighty-one more games to play?"

If you looked past Johnson's beatific grin, you saw a grim competitor who could and would do anything to win. "There is no question in my mind that Magic is the best player in the game and the best player I've ever seen," said no less an authority than the Boston Celtics' Larry Bird, a three-time NBA MVP. "He plays the game the way I like to see people play, and the way I like to play. He passes, rebounds, leads. Whatever it takes, that's what he does to win."

Indeed, the bottom line is winning, and Johnson paid strict attention to that column in the standings. He led Michigan State University to the NCAA championship as a sophomore in 1979. And the Los Angeles Lakers reached the NBA finals eight times in the first ten seasons of Johnson's professional career, winning five titles. "I may not be the greatest," Johnson says, "but I've got a whole lot more diamonds [championship rings] than a lot of guys who play this game. Winning is

© Stephen Dunn/Allsport

It doesn't get any better than this at point guard. Here, the Los Angeles Lakers' Magic Johnson surveys the court with Kevin Edwards of the Miami Heat providing token resistance.

© Brian Drake/Sportschrome East/West

what it's all about. That's how I want to be remembered."

In the 1980s, the Lakers thrived with Johnson at the point. Making players around him better is something that always marked Johnson's performances. And it wasn't just passing to Abdul-Jabbar. Johnson somehow managed to complement disparate players like Jamaal Wilkes, Norm Nixon, Byron Scott, A.C. Green, and James Worthy.

Compare Johnson's assists-per-game figures to those of history's giants at point guard, Oscar Robertson and Bob Cousy. Johnson's career average for each forty-eight minutes is a stunning 14.6. Cousy (11.1) and Robertson (10.8) aren't even close. How about rebounds? Johnson's full-game projected average of 9.6 is better than Robertson's 8.5.

Each off-season, Johnson took a facet of his game and tried to perfect it: three-point shots (his accuracy, once around 20 percent, was 38.4 percent in 1989–90), free-throw shooting (once 76 percent from the line, Johnson averaged about 90 percent in 1988–89 and 1989–90), and scoring (Johnson averaged about eighteen points per game, but later that figure

crept up to around twenty-two points per game).

Johnson's work ethic can be traced to his father, Earvin, Sr., whom Johnson credited in his autobiography, *Magic's Touch*. Johnson wrote, "If it was summer, my dad would make me take that lawn mower around and cut yards for money. If it was winter, I took the snow shovel and felt like I was clearing the whole neighborhood. But no matter what I did, I never worked as hard as my dad did. How important was it to me that he got up and worked two jobs every day? Very important, because that's the motivation I used from the time I started playing basketball."

Running the show. That's what Magic Johnson did. When the coach draws up the plays on the sideline, the number he gives to the point guard is number one. This is no accident. Seeing the whole court, the other nine players, at all times, is the job of the point guard. He generally brings the ball up court and handles it more often than any player, thus exerting more control and impact on a game. As University of Connecticut coach Jim Calhoun says, "The guy who has the ball determines what's going to happen in the game."

With the introduction of the shot clock and the three-point shot, the point guard's importance has increased. Not only must a point guard distribute the ball wisely and efficiently to his teammates, but he must also be versatile enough to play defense, rebound on occasion, take the ball to the basket quickly and with abandon, and penetrate when the opening presents itself. By drawing the wide bodies of the paint to him, the point guard creates scoring opportunities for others. Not to mention for himself.

Many of the NBA's younger fans might think that Johnson invented the triple-double, the rare feat of averaging double digits for points, rebounds, and assists. For one incredible season, 1961–62, Oscar Robertson averaged a triple-double—30.8 points, 12.5 rebounds, and 11.4 assists. Johnson passed Robertson in 1990–91 when he raised his career assists to 9,921. However, John Stockton may soon come to rank alongside Robertson and Johnson.

Stockton played college ball in the relative obscurity of Gonzaga University in Spokane, Washington, after a high school career at Gonzaga Prep. A six-foot-one (185-cm), 175-pound (79-kg) guard, Stockton was the sixteenth choice of the Utah Jazz in the first round of the 1984 draft. In retrospect, he should have been at the head of the pack. Bobby Knight was similarly mistaken when he selected the 1984 U.S. Olympic team and left Stockton off the roster. "I guess people didn't want to take what I accomplished there very seriously because Spokane doesn't have much of a reputation of throwing out a lot of great basketball players," Stockton says.

It does now. After three middling seasons in the NBA, Stockton blossomed into one of the game's premier point guards. In 1987–88, he set the all-time single-season record for assists, with 1,128. After missing that standard by only ten the following season, Stockton dished the ball 1,134 times in 1989–90, to break his own record—a feat accomplished in four fewer games. Then in 1990–91, he broke his own record again, recording 1,164 assists. That gave Stockton four of the five best assist totals in history. His average per game in 1989–90 was a staggering 14.5. The next best totals? Detroit's Isiah Thomas handed out 13.9 per game in 1984–85, and Stockton has the next two, 13.8 in 1987–88 and 13.6 a season later. In 1993, Stockton and Thomas became the third and fourth players in NBA history to achieve 8,000 assists. Stockton won his sixth consecutive assists title with an average of 12.0 per game.

At the same time, Stockton's intuition and anticipation allowed him to steal the ball 207 times in 1989–90, the league's second-best (2.65) average per game behind Chicago's Michael Jordan. The year before, Stockton became the third player to lead the NBA in assists and steals (3.2 per game).

Point guards are also measured by how they protect the basketball—not allowing anyone to take it away. No one does that better than Stockton. In 1989–90, for instance, his 1,134 assists and 207 steals were balanced by only 272 turnovers. That's a ratio of 4 to 9. By comparison, Magic Johnson's ratio of assists and steals to turnovers was 3 to 6. Because of his size, Stockton cannot score and rebound the way Johnson does, but he has worked hard to become an offensive factor. He averaged more than seventeen points per game in 1988–89 and 1989–90, and his career shooting percentage is an impressive 52.4. In a showdown with Johnson in the 1988 NBA playoffs, Stockton equaled Johnson's post-season, single-game record of twenty-four assists. He also set records for a seven-game series with 115 assists and twenty-eight steals.

Stockton seems uncomfortable talking about his achieve-

ments. "I'm not the best athlete in the league or the most skilled guy," he says. "I can't get away with trying to be tricky. I leave that to the big moves that come after the pass. My feet are firmly on the ground. Having gone to Gonzaga, you learn humility. But most of all you learn to compete against people who are better than you and have a lot of fun doing it."

Third among NBA point guards in 1989–90 was Kevin Johnson of the Phoenix Suns. "He has the bored look of a guy painting a fence when he's on the court," wrote Jim Murray, the Pulitzer Prize-winning columnist for the *Los Angeles Times*. Johnson begs to differ. "It's concentration, really," he says.

Johnson, who is four years younger than Stockton, offers a rare balance of shooting and passing. In 1989–90, he averaged 22.5 points and 11.4 assists. In doing so, he joined only four other players in NBA history to average more than twenty points and ten assists for a season—Oscar Robertson, Magic Johnson, Isiah Thomas, and Nate Archibald.

Johnson was the seventh player taken in the 1987 college draft, out of the University of California at Berkeley. He was only six foot one (185 cm) and 190 pounds (86 kg), but his acceleration and quickness were astonishing. The Cleveland Cavaliers played the rookie only twenty-four minutes a game, and not surprisingly, Johnson averaged only 7.3 points and 3.7 assists backing up Mark Price in fifty-two games. On February 25, 1988, Johnson was dealt to Phoenix with Mark West, Tyrone Corbin, the Cavs' 1988 first- and second-round draft choices, plus the second pick in 1989, in exchange for Larry Nance, Mike Sanders, and the Suns' 1988 second-round pick. In the twenty-eight games Johnson played in Phoenix, he averaged 12.6 points and 8.7 assists. Johnson was named the NBA's April Rookie of the Month, but larger things awaited him.

"I think I was a little different than most of the guys," Johnson says. "I never really had any expectations of playing in the pros. I generally took things one step at a time, from high school to college. It wasn't until my senior year, when I scored twenty-six points in a half against Stanford, that I started thinking maybe I had a shot at the NBA. From that point on, I really started focusing on it, working toward it."

Johnson says that his concentration on defense gained the attention of professional scouts. "Being a point guard and wanting to be like Maurice Cheeks, I realized I better start paying attention to that. So I concentrated on defense. It

The "other" Johnson, Kevin Johnson of the Phoenix Suns, is one of the game's premier point guards.

wasn't that I was so good at it, it was just total will and desire."

Johnson averaged more than thirty-nine minutes each game for the Suns in 1988–89 and produced averages of 20.4 points and 12.2 assists. He was named the NBA's Most Improved Player. Johnson is a good shooter, both from the field (he was 50 percent his last two seasons) and the foul line, where his career average approaches 86 percent.

The heir-apparent to the throne of Johnson, Johnson, and Stockton may well be Golden State's Tim Hardaway. In 1989–90, he and San Antonio Spurs center David Robinson were the

© Ken Levine/Allsport

only unanimous choices to the NBA's All-Rookie Team. Hardaway is listed at six feet even (183 cm) and 175 pounds (19 kg), but he is closer to five foot eleven (180 cm). In his first professional season, Hardaway averaged 14.7 points and 8.7 assists. In his second season, he was selected to play in the league All-Star Game—to the credit of his deadly crossover dribble. Hardaway dribbles the ball between his legs from his right hand to his left, then once in front, from left to right. The move routinely freezes NBA guards as Hardaway moves to the basket. "It's bang, bang, and you're dead," says Magic Johnson. Hardaway's first four seasons in the league produced a 9.7 assists per game average, and in 1992–93 he was the only player other than Stockton to average double figures in assists (10.6).

Point guard Isiah Thomas has been killing them softly since he arrived in the NBA in 1981 after lifting Indiana University to the NCAA title. Thomas' career averages of 9.7 assists and 19.8 points per game are among the best of all time. As the Detroit Pistons improved around him, the pressure lessened for Thomas to carry the team himself. Consider the facts: In eleven college and professional seasons, Thomas won three championships. In 1989–90, the Pistons became the third team in NBA history to win consecutive titles. And although Thomas did not have the glittering numbers he has had in previous post-season play, he was truly the Pistons' point guard. With his multilevel contributions in the playoffs—20.5 points per game and 8.2 assists, plus 5.5 rebounds and 2.2 steals—he ran the show.

Mark Price, who was traded to the Cleveland Cavaliers for Kevin Johnson, is another premier point guard. He is listed at six foot one (185 cm), but he may not clear six feet (183 cm). Critics said he was too small to play NBA basketball. Too slow, too. But he could pass and shoot, and he was tough. After a terrific career at Georgia Tech, Price was chosen in the second round of the 1986 draft, twenty-fifth by the Dallas Mavericks. Before the season began, the Mavericks dealt Price to the Cavaliers for a future second-rounder and cash. After limited duty as a rookie, Price flourished, averaging eighteen points a game the next three years, and nine assists per game the past two. "I think I've broken ground," Price says. "It's not as hard for little guys to break through and get respect in the game anymore. It feels good when you go beyond perceptions."

While Isiah Thomas has developed a reputation off the court for being self-centered, on the court he can be a giving human being . . . to the tune of nearly ten assists per game. It's no accident that his teams have won an NCAA title and two NBA crowns.

**Even sophisticated double- and triple-team defenses haven't held Michael Jordan down. Through 1990–91, he had led the NBA in scoring five years running, a feat only Wilt Chamberlain surpassed.**

# THE SHOOTING GUARD (2)

How does one quantify a Michael Jeffrey Jordan? Not very easily, for numbers fall short of capturing basketball's most exciting player. Most of the game's searing scorers are big men, but Jordan has the modest dimensions of a shooting guard. Still, the six-foot-six (198-cm), 198-pound (90-kg) package consistently rises above his peers. In fact, at the age of twenty-eight, Jordan is shooting against NBA history as much as against opponents.

Consider the riches he has wrought:

• Jordan finished his 1992–93 season with the Chicago Bulls averaging 32.6 points per game, a figure good enough to lead the league—for the seventh season in a row. Only the towering Wilt Chamberlain managed that, from 1960–67.

• Jordan's scoring average through nine professional seasons, 32.29 points, is the highest in professional history. Chamberlain's best was 30.1. Jordan and Chamberlain are the only two players in league history to score more than 3,000 points in a single season.

• In the crucible of the playoffs, nobody does it better than Jordan. In more than 100 playoff games, Jordan's average is 34.6 points. He averaged 41 points per game in the 1993 NBA final series, a record, and won the Most Valuable Player award in the finals for the third consecutive year. A distant second on the all-time list is Los Angeles Lakers guard Jerry West, at 29.1. Jordan's sixty-three-point performance against Boston, on April 20, 1986, set the NBA standard.

• Jordan was named the NBA's Defensive Player of the Year in 1988 and made the All-Defensive first team in 1988, 1989, and 1990. Jordan has led the league twice in steals, and his average per game (2.8) is the highest in league history.

• Over the 1986–87 season, Jordan made 236 steals and blocked 125 shots. He became the first player in league history to clear 200 steals and 100 blocked shots, and the blocked shots were the most ever by a guard. Also during that season, on April 16, Jordan pumped in twenty-three straight points against the Atlanta Hawks—another record.

"It must be like the rest of us playing with grade-school kids," says Chicago Bulls teammate John Paxson. "That's how good he is."

© Stephen Dunn/Allsport

Not only can "Air" Jordan soar to the basket, correct himself in mid-course, and throw down thunderous jams, he can work himself free under the basket for his classic reverse layups, *and* he can shoot. His wondrous leaping ability and acceleration make it all happen. In 1989–90, he added an accurate long-range jump shot to his arsenal, making him the toughest guard in history. If defenders back toward the basket, Jordan shoots over them. If they are bold and press him too closely, he is past them for an easy two points. Obviously, Jordan is more than just a shooting guard. He plays the passing lanes as well as anyone on defense. And offense? Through 1989–90, Jordan had achieved the so-called triple-double twenty-one times. Against Portland on February 23, 1990, for instance, he produced thirty-five points, ten rebounds, and ten assists. When he played point guard for the Bulls for a brief spell in 1990, Jordan averaged 10.8 assists per game. There are times when Jordan and the Bulls wish he didn't have to do everything, because he is essentially a one-man team.

These days, no one hangs in the air longer than Michael Jordan. His majestic drives to the basket can be breathtaking.

**Finally, after six frustrating seasons, Michael Jordan removed the only burden of his professional career. He and the Chicago Bulls won the NBA title in 1990–91. After it was over, Jordan, tears in his eyes, embraced the trophy and his dreams.**

© Ken Levine/Allsport

"All I ask of my players is to put us in position to win after three quarters," says Chicago coach Doug Collins. "If we can accomplish that, then Jordan can do the rest. I doubt there ever has been a better closer than Michael."

When power forward Charles Oakley was traded to the New York Knicks in 1988, Jordan lost a valuable ally. Oakley's physical presence took some of the pressure off Jordan. Without Oakley, Jordan was forced to crash opposing defenses early and often, and there is evidence that the physical toll is exacting a price. The minutes he plays each game (38.7 through seven seasons) and the way he plays defense don't allow Jordan much time to rest. Afterall, he is not large by NBA standards and the amount of time he controls the ball clearly wears on him. If he continues at this pace, his career may be cut short by the abuse his body suffers. Jordan tries not to think about it too much. "I'm a young thoroughbred," he says, "and young thoroughbreds don't need rest."

His game is already changing, and he is becoming more well-rounded for it, if that is possible. Fewer are the bone-rattling excursions to the basket; more often Jordan pulls up and hits his soft-as-silk jump shot.

This kind of versatility seemed farfetched when Jordan was trying to make the varsity basketball team at Laney High School in Wilmington, North Carolina. That's right, trying. In one of the most celebrated stories in basketball, he did not make the team on his first attempt! LeRoy Smith made it ahead of Jordan, and Jordan never has forgotten.

"Being cut definitely had a big effect on me," Jordan says. "It was embarrassing, not making the team. They posted the roster in the locker room, and it was there for a long, long time without my name on it. I remember being really mad, too, because there was a guy who made it that really wasn't as good as me. I was down about not making it for a while, and I thought about not playing anymore. Of course, I did keep playing, and whenever I was working out and got tired, figured I ought to stop, I'd close my eyes and see that list in the locker room without my name on it. That got me going again."

Jordan was a winner at North Carolina, where the Tar Heels won an NCAA championship in 1982 when he was a freshman. North Carolina was ranked first in the nation by the Associated Press in two of Jordan's three seasons there. He left a year early and was the NBA's Rookie of the Year in 1985. The Chicago Bulls, 27–55 before he arrived, improved to 38–44 and made the playoffs for the first time in four years. By 1987–88, the Bulls had become a 50–32 team, and today Chicago stands astride the NBA as 1990–91 champions.

Good shooting guards provide points like their front-line counterparts at finesse forward. The great ones, like Jordan and Portland's Clyde "The Glide" Drexler, do more than torch opponents with twenty points of instant offense each game. Drexler, at six foot seven (201 cm), 215 pounds (97 kg), is a deceptively productive rebounder for a guard. Over a seven-year career, Drexler has pulled down 3,305 rebounds for an average of six per game. He can pass too, averaging 5.6 assists per game. And defense? How about 2.3 steals per game?

Because he was a glamorous player at the University of Houston, Drexler has always been perceived as a scorer. Playing forward next to center Hakeem Olajuwon, Drexler helped carry Houston to the NCAA Final Four two years in a row. He averaged 15.9 points and 8.8 rebounds as a junior before deciding to turn professional in 1983. After a rookie season of adjustment, Drexler was ready to make an impression on the NBA, with an assist from Julius Erving. "I always set out to be the best," Drexler says, "but I didn't always know quite what that meant. Achieving the maximum potential in school turned out to be a lot different than doing that in the NBA. I realized that the first time I met Julius Erving. He was my idol, he was 'The Man.' Moses Malone introduced me to him after a Rockets game one night. He was just as great a player in person as he was on television, but it was more than that. He was so personable, so interested in what I had to say. He was a special person with special talents, and I started thinking, 'If I could ever be like that . . .'

"Julius talked a lot that night about giving your best, on and off the floor. Ever since then, it's been a simple rule for me. It's a question of wanting to be the best."

Drexler averaged 27.0 points in 1987–88 and followed that up with a 27.2 point average a season later. Through eight seasons, he is averaging 20.5 points per game to go with his other contributions. Drexler, supported by Buck Williams, Terry Porter, and Kevin Duckworth in Portland, may help bring the championship that eluded him in Houston to the Trail Blazers.

Although Joe Dumars III does not sport the classic numbers of a top-notch shooting guard, he ranks among the NBA's best because he scores when the Detroit Pistons need a boost. He also plays defense with abandon, a rare two-way combination. Dumars is not big—only six foot three (190 cm) and 190 pounds (86 kg), but he was a terrific college player. In 1985, he became the eleventh leading scorer in NCAA history by averaging 22.5 points per game for McNeese State University in Lake Charles, Louisiana. The Pistons selected him eighteenth overall in the 1985 draft, seeing him as a role player who could score and play defense in the limited time he would see. And so, Dumars averaged only twenty-four minutes a game as a rookie. The patience he learned as the youngest of six boys and the last of seven children helped him cope as teammate Isiah Thomas ran the show for Detroit.

During the 1988–89 season, however, Dumars was finally recognized as one of the game's great players. He was never spectacular; just consistently versatile. He averaged 17.2 points per game over the regular season and usually suffocated the opposing team's best-shooting guard. Dumars was named to the NBA's All-Defensive first team that year, but his major contribution came in the playoffs. In Game Two of the finals against the Lakers, Dumars scored twenty-six first-half points to keep the Pistons in a game they might otherwise have lost. In Game Three, Dumars scored twenty-one points in the third quarter, including a dazzling run of seventeen in a row. He averaged 27.3 in the Pistons' unlikely sweep of the two-time defending champion Lakers. Not even Thomas could overshadow that performance. Dumars was named the playoffs' MVP, joining others like James Worthy, Magic Johnson, Larry Bird, Moses Malone, and Kareem Abdul-Jabbar.

What is it like to score seventeen consecutive points in an NBA playoff final series? "When you're shooting that well, you feel like you're detached, away from the game," says Dumars, who shot 58 percent in the series. "As soon as you get the ball, you just let it go, so that it just barely passes through your hands."

The 1989–90 season was virtually an instant replay for Dumars. He averaged a career-best 17.8 points per game and improved on that number (18.2) in the playoffs. He wasn't the Pistons' MVP in their five-game victory over Portland in the finals, but there were extenuating circumstances. Dumars led all scorers with thirty-three points in Game Three, but that day his father died. Dumars considered leaving the team to go home, but his mother convinced him to stay. He averaged seventeen points in the next two games as Detroit wrapped up its second consecutive championship.

**Lost in the wake of Michael Jordan is Clyde "The Glide" Drexler, the wondrous shooting guard for the Portland Trail Blazers. Through his career, night after night, he has been an automatic 20-point scorer.**

Dumars, polite and unassuming, has managed to stay that way against all odds. "All of this reaffirms my life values and the way I was raised, what I was taught to believe in," Dumars says. "And I can say that it pays to work hard and do the right thing. Because you can reap the benefits."

Scan the NBA's top ten scoring list for 1989–90 and you will find the familiar names: Jordan, Malone, Ewing, Chambers, Barkley, and Miller. Miller? That's right, Reggie Miller of the Indiana Pacers averaged 24.6 points per game. Previously, he was almost better known for being the brother of USC basketball All-America Cheryl Miller. Not anymore.

Miller, a lean six foot seven (198 cm) and 190 pounds (86 kg), was a lights-out shooter at UCLA, where he shot 54.7 percent from the field. Success came more slowly at the professional level. Miller averaged thirteen points per game his first two seasons before his "coming-out" in 1989–90. His three-point shot improved dramatically; Miller sank 41.4 percent of his long-range bombs. He made his first All-Star Game as well, and clearly, it won't be his last.

If Dumars and Miller were once underrated shooting guards, what does that make Lafayette "Fat" Lever? Here is a listed six-foot-three (190-cm) (six-foot-one [185-cm], actually), 175-pound (79-kg) (maybe) player who literally does everything. In 1989–90 he not only scored 1,443 points, for an average of 18.3 per game, but added 734 rebounds (9.3), 517 assists (6.5), and 168 steals (2.1). He was the only guard other than Washington's Darrell Walker to rank among the league's top twenty in rebounds, assists, and steals. Lever remains the only player in NBA history listed at six-foot-three or smaller to come down with six hundred or more rebounds for four straight seasons. He is also the fifth guard in history to average more than nine rebounds per game and the others, including Oscar Robertson and Magic Johnson, were far taller.

Lever, who has played in Portland, Denver, and now plays in Dallas, is not a typical shooting guard who fires away from the periphery. He manages to slip in amongst the trees in the paint and score his points in creative ways. Still, it is his rebounding that astounds the players. "A lot of rebounding is instinct," says Doug Moe, Lever's coach in Denver. "But you have to want to go in and do it. The key thing about Fat is that he's mentally tough. Everyone lets up sometimes. It's natural. But I've never seen Fat let up. He is the ultimate competitor."

© Brian Drake/Sportschrome East/West

Three more names for consideration: Detroit's Vinnie "The Microwave" Johnson, Cleveland's Ron Harper, and Hersey Hawkins of Philadelphia. Johnson, who is a stocky six foot two (188 cm) and 200 pounds (91 kg), is a veteran of eleven NBA seasons. He has never been an All-Star nor ranked among the top ten scorers. He is a specialist. He's a scorer, and like a microwave, he offers instant results. "Yes," Johnson says, "I'm a scorer, not a shooter. I need minutes, but sometimes I don't get them. But this team knows that when it's on the line, I'll be there and I'll come through for them." With Dumars and Thomas, Johnson's presence gives the Pistons one of the best-balanced guard units in history.

**He is not as flashy as his backcourt mate Isiah Thomas, but Joe Dumars is clearly just as valuable. His defense is unimpeachable and so is his ability to score under duress.**

© Damian Strohmeyer/Allsport

**Before his serious knee injury, Bernard King was lethal on the fastbreak. Afterward, he developed his inside game and regained his uncanny shooting touch.**

Harper and Hawkins are names for the future. Harper averaged nearly twenty points per game in four seasons for Miami of Ohio and led the Cavaliers with a 22.0 point scoring average in 1989–90. Hawkins is a pure scorer. He led all NCAA Division I scorers in 1990, averaging 36.3 points per game at Bradley University and pushed his NBA average to 18.5 points in his second season with the 76ers. Hawkins' career shooting percentage is a queasy 45.8, but his philosophy is the same one that keeps all shooting guards going through bad times: Keep shooting and sooner or later something will fall.

## THE SMALL (FINESSE) FORWARD (3)

In many ways, the term small forward is misleading. Finesse is probably a more accurate term. In today's professional game, there are some so-called small forwards who approach seven feet (213 cm) in height.

While power forwards are expected to rebound, finesse forwards play in the corners and have three duties: score, score, and score. They are generally smaller than power forwards and quicker, too. Most of the good ones have more than one way to score, be it shooting a jump shot, slicing to the basket, or maneuvering in close with a host of subtle moves. Defense is not a prerequisite.

Of the top ten scorers in professional history (ABA and NBA combined), four can be classified as finesse forwards: Julius Erving (30,026 points, for an average of 24.2), George Gervin (26,595 points, 25.1), John Havlicek (26,395 points, 20.8), and Rick Barry (25,279 points, 24.8).

In many ways, Bernard King, at six feet seven (201 cm) and 205 pounds (93 kg), is a classic finesse forward. In thirteen fragmented seasons, he scored 19,432 points, twenty-first on the all-time NBA list, and averaged 23.1 points per game.

When the NBA All-Stars were introduced to the jam-packed crowd at the Charlotte Coliseum on February 10, 1991, the biggest ovation was for thirty-four-year-old Bernard King. He stood there at mid-court with a goofy smile on his face—his trademark scowl was nowhere to be seen. Six years earlier, King had been an All-Star. In fact, the New York Knicks' small forward was leading the league in scoring at the time with an average of 32.9 points per game. However, after a disaster on March 23, 1985, King was probably the only person who thought he might return to that position of eminence.

"This is a great, great feeling," he said at an emotional press conference before the All-Star Game. "I've been waiting for this feeling for six years. This is the culmination of a dream. I've always believed in myself; I never doubted my ability to come back. I've labored for six years, and I deserve this. When I think back to the many hours I spent working in my basement on a daily basis, to the doctors who told me I would never play again, to all the naysayers who said I would never reach this level again. . . ."

King couldn't finish the sentence. He began to weep. His personal triumph is a moving story. Six years earlier, King went up to block a shot by Kansas City's Reggie Theus, and when he hit the hardwood, the anterior cruciate ligament in his right knee snapped like a twig. In light of other players' experiences with such an injury, his NBA career seemed finished. A day later, King lay stretched out in his bed at Lenox

Hill Hospital in New York and studied literature on reconstruction of the anterior cruciate, the knee's primary hinge. He interviewed specialists, and only two doctors (one being Knicks team physician Dr. Norman Scott) dared to suggest he might play again—and they didn't say anything about the All-Star Game. King underwent reconstructive surgery, which was deemed a success; the rehabilitation was up to King.

"I guess you have to understand that the injury I was recovering from was so severe that, at that point, nobody had ever come back to successfully play at their same level," King says. "In the public's mind or in terms of the media or in terms of the doctors, the question wasn't, 'Would he come back and be an All-Star?' The question wasn't, 'Well, what kind of player would he be?' The question was, 'Would he come back?'

"Well, I didn't want to limit myself. If I was going to rehab my knee, I was going to completely rehab my knee and be everything I used to be."

In six months, after teaching himself how to swim in order to speed the knee's recovery, King could walk with leg weights. In a year, he was back running in the gym. By the end of the 1986–87 season, after two years of working five hours a day, seven days a week, he was given clearance to return to the NBA. King played in six games that season. Wearing a cumbersome knee brace, he averaged 22.7 points.

He had played only those six games in two seasons when the Knicks let him slip away. King signed with the Washington Bullets as a free agent before the 1987 season. He struggled when the knee sometimes failed to make the slashing, gliding bursts he had been able to make to the basket for the Knicks. For a few seasons in New York, King had been virtually unstoppable. His explosion to the basket was awesome; it was like watching a man soar up a ramp, high above the floor. Over time, King's knee grew stronger. He adjusted to compensate. Instead of flying to the basket for a slam dunk or lay-in, he perfected his fall-away jump shot and took more shots from ten to twelve feet. The ball still went in. His average per game climbed from 17.2 points in 1987–88 to 20.7 points to 22.4 points in 1989–90. He was the only Bullets player to start each of the team's eighty-two games that season. It was the first time he had done that since the 1978–79 season.

King actually led the league in scoring early in the 1990–91 season. In January, he scored fifty-two points against the Denver Nuggets. Two days earlier he had torched his old teammates with forty-nine points before family and friends in Madison Square Garden. King was third in scoring with an average of 29.9, behind Michael Jordan and Charles Barkley. Starting for the Eastern Conference All-Stars, King played twenty-six minutes and produced eight points and three rebounds. Modest numbers, perhaps, but King was truly happy to be there. His peers seemed to understand the magnitude of his achievement.

"Anyone who can recover from that type of injury deserves to become a starter on the All-Star team: he must be one of the strongest individuals on the face of the earth," said the Los Angeles Lakers' Magic Johnson. "He can conquer anything. See, you've got to realize how much inner strength that takes. That's what I look for in a person, inner strength, and Bernard King is one of my personal heroes."

Julius Erving, "Dr. J" to the world, is probably the role model for the finesse forward, the seminal figure for today's pure scorer. "Doc was the first guy to fly," says Kevin Loughery, who coached Erving when he played for the New Jersey Nets of the ABA. "He did things with a basketball that nobody else had ever done. I honestly believe that Doc did more for pro basketball than anybody, on and off the court."

Actually, the six-foot-seven (201-cm), 210-pound (95-kg) Erving could play pretty fair defense as well. He is also professional basketball's leader in all-time steals (2,272) and seventh with 1,941 blocked shots. But his soaring, swooping 30,026 points are the things people remember. Actually, most of today's finesse forwards have the versatility to excel at various facets of the game. Larry Bird, at the advanced age of thirty-four, probably comes closest to defining the position today—though *finesse* is a word with which he is hardly familiar. Still, scoring is the thing he does best—or at least the most often.

Ask Red Auerbach (who is, admittedly, biased) who he'd take first in a match game of all-time NBA stars. "If I had to start a team," says the Boston Celtics' president, "the one guy in all of history I would take is Larry Bird. This is the greatest ball player who ever played the game."

This statement was not made lightly; Auerbach deeply appreciated the impact Celtics center Bill Russell had on the game. But look at the facts. Before Bird, the Celtics went

**Previous page: The stylish Clyde Drexler of the Portland Trail Blazers is just another example of why the NBA boasts the finest athletes in professional sports.**

29–53 in 1978–79. In Bird's first season, 1979–80, the Celtics were 61–21. Boston never suffered a losing month until the 1988–89 season, when Bird was sidelined with an injury.

Bird grew up in French Lick, Indiana, and made the freshman team at Springs Valley High School, in part, because his father promised him twenty dollars if he did. He would practice for three hours at the high school, then try to walk past the basketball court fifty feet from his grandmother's house. "The guys were always out there playing," remembers Bird. "I was tired and cold and hungry. So when they asked me to play, I'd say, 'No.' Then they'd say, 'What's the matter, you're too good to play with us?' They were all about four, five, six years older than me. A lot of times, I didn't even want to play because it was winter and it was really cold out. But I kind of had to. After a while, I got used to it. Looking back, nothing seemed so hard after those days back when I was in high school."

At six foot nine (206 cm), 220 pounds (100 kg), Bird had the intelligence, vision, and passing skills to play point guard. Sure, he was slow of foot and no one ever saw him jump more than a foot off the ground, but he played an essential role when the Celtics needed it. Yet, Bird was more valuable as the versatile finesse forward, the counterpart to six-foot-ten (208-cm) Kevin McHale. First, Bird was a scorer. After his retirement following the 1991–92 season, Bird had scored 21,791 points, ranking eleventh on the NBA-ABA list, an average of 24.3 per game. In his thirteen seasons, Bird also averaged 10.0 rebounds, 6.3 assists, and 1.73 steals per game. He shot 50 percent from the floor and 88 percent from the free-throw line. Bird led the league in free-throw percentage four different times. In 1986–87, Bird became the first player in league history to shoot 50 percent from the floor (52.5) and 90 percent (91.0) from the line. He did it again the next season. The Bird legend grew when he won the All-Star Game's three-point contest in the first three years of its existence. This was more a tribute to his poise under pressure and competitive spirit than his natural shooting ability.

Auerbach and the Celtics drafted Bird sixth overall as a junior eligible in the 1978 draft. After his Indiana State team lost to Magic Johnson's Michigan State club in the NCAA final in 1979, he joined the Celtics and turned the franchise around. Bird has always done what is necessary in a given game. He has an awareness of players on the court that rivals Johnson's. In each of his first nine seasons, he was named to the All-NBA First Team. He was the regular-season MVP three years running—1984, 1985, and 1986—something only two players (Wilt Chamberlain and Bill Russell) had done before him. Bird carried Boston to three NBA championships and won MVP honors twice.

Bird had to miss all but six games in the 1988–89 season, when bone spurs were removed from both his heels. When he returned, his mobility wasn't quite the same and his shooting percentage dipped slightly. Still, Bird came back with a 24.3 point average and his 562 assists were the second-highest total of his career. "I had some major surgery and I have to live with what I got," said Bird with typical stoicism.

Was he worried about the criticism of the Celtics' aging front line, which featured Bird (thirty-four), McHale (thirty-three), and center Robert Parish (thirty-seven)?

"Hey," Bird said, sounding feisty, "we still play better than any rookie that comes into the league, and ninety percent of the veterans. So, no, we don't worry about that too much."

Conjure up a picture of the prototypical finesse forward: He is six foot eight (203 cm), 200 pounds (91 kg). Fast. Smooth. Has a million moves. Jumps to the moon. He is exciting, he is ... why, Jacques Dominique Wilkins, "The Human Highlight Film."

He exploded out of the University of Georgia after three seasons and was the third pick in the 1982 draft. The Utah Jazz dealt him to the Atlanta Hawks for John Drew, Freeman Williams, and a wad of cash. Atlanta got the better end of the deal. Wilkins averaged only 17.5 points per game as a rookie, but many of those points were scored in spectacular, slam-dunk fashion. As his confidence and experience grew, Wilkins' scoring average increased. In 1985–86, he averaged 30.3 points per game, enough to lead the NBA. Wilkins was the last man to lead the league in scoring before Michael Jordan of the Chicago Bulls made that category his personal showcase. And those who criticize Wilkins for not rebounding (he has a respectable 7.0 per game) or playing defense, miss the point. Wilkins gives his team a scoring presence, which is something not many people can do. Through eight seasons, Wilkins had scored 16,695 points. His average of 26.1 points per game is sixth on the all-time professional list.

James Worthy of the Los Angeles Lakers, at six foot nine (206 cm), 225 pounds (102 kg), is one of the league's perennial stars at finesse forward. In 1990–91, he was selected to play in his sixth consecutive All-Star Game. Like Bird and Johnson, he is a winner. His North Carolina team, which included a freshman named Michael Jordan, won the 1982 NCAA championship. Worthy scored a game-high twenty-eight points in the 63–62 victory over Georgetown in the final. With Worthy in the lineup, the Lakers won three NBA titles—four championships in seven years. Moreover, Worthy rises to the playoff occasion. In 1982, he was named the NCAA Division I Tournament's Most Outstanding Player. Six years later, he was the NBA playoff MVP when he averaged 21.1 points in twenty-four post-season games. He had thirty-six points in Game Seven of the final when the Lakers beat the Detroit Pistons. Worthy's game is built on acceleration to the basket and some marvelous moves once he gets there. While Wilkins, for instance, has a career shooting average of 47 percent, Worthy, who is far more judicious in his shot selection, averages 54.6 percent.

Chris Mullin is the quintessential gym rat. Born in New York City, he played high school ball at Xaverian in Brooklyn, and later graduated to St. John's University, New York. Long after practice was over, you could find him alone in the gym

**Don't look now, but Larry Bird of the Boston Celtics is about to exploit this double-team with one of his patented over-the-head passes to a teammate.**

shooting baskets. He had his own set of keys. Mullin, six foot seven (200 cm), 215 pounds (97 kg), played on the gold-medal-winning 1984 U.S. Olympic basketball team. The Golden State Warriors, seemingly unconcerned with Mullin's lack of speed, made him the seventh choice in the 1985 draft.

"I think even up to now, a lot of people through high school and college thought I was too slow," says Mullin, who looks to Bird as a role model. "They always talked about how I couldn't move, couldn't jump. It didn't make me mad, and it wasn't like this constant thing that pushed me, but looking back, it was definitely an obstacle to cross. All through high school, I was just a good shooter. I started to realize if I could shoot and handle the ball, then I could drive. If I could drive, then I might get fouled, but that wasn't going to be worth anything unless I could shoot free throws."

Through seven seasons, Mullin was averaging 22.5 points per game with a shooting percentage of 51.8 and a free-throw percentage of 87.2. The 1991 All-Star Game was his third straight in a row.

The leading scorer among finesse forwards over the 1989–90 season was Tom Chambers of the Phoenix Suns. At six foot ten (208 cm) and 230 pounds (106 kg), Chambers is surprisingly delicate around the basket. After hovering around the twenty-point mark for the first seven years of his career in San Diego and Seattle, Chambers broke through in Phoenix. He averaged 25.7 points in 1988–89 and set a Suns record with 2,085 points that year. A year later he produced 27.2 points per game and a new record total of 2,201 points. Chambers was the MVP of the 1987 All-Star Game when he scored thirty-four points against the best of his peers.

Another finesse forward to watch is Xavier McDaniel, the "X Man," who averaged more than twenty points per game in the first five seasons of his career. At six foot six (198 cm), 209 pounds (95 kg), he is almost wispy to look at, but he plays like iron. In 1985, playing for Wichita State University, he became the second man only to lead all NCAA Division I players in both scoring and rebounding (27.2 and 14.8 per game). When the Phoenix Suns traded for McDaniel early in the 1990–91 season, they hoped he, along with Chambers, was the missing piece to the championship puzzle. "All my life I've felt I had to

© David L. Johnson/Sportschrome East/West

prove myself to people," McDaniel says. "I wasn't nothing coming out of high school. And even when I was a little kid playing street basketball against older guys, they would always intimidate me. Now, I'm not afraid of anybody."

No list of finesse forwards could exclude the venerable Alex English. Through fifteen seasons he has scored an amazing 25,613 points and averaged 21.5 points per game. He trails only Moses Malone on the list of active scorers. English, a lean six foot seven (201 cm) and 190 pounds (86 kg), found his scoring touch in Denver, for whom he played in eight consecutive All-Star Games.

Once known as "The Human Highlight Film," Dominique Wilkins (*left*) of the Atlanta Hawks has worked hard to improve his rebounding and defense. Meanwhile, Chicago's Scottie Pippen (inset) can handle the ball as well as pull up for a deadly twelve-foot shot.

# THE POWER FORWARD (4)

paint (pānt): 1. a) to make (a picture, design, etc.) in colors applied to a surface; b) to depict or portray with paints; 2. to describe colorfully or vividly; depict in words; 3. to cover or decorate with paint; 4. to apply cosmetics to; adorn; beautify.

That's the generic definition, according to Webster's Dictionary. Ask Karl Malone of the Utah Jazz about the paint—the sixteen-feet-by-eighteen-feet-ten-inch (4.9-m-by-5.7-m) lane under the basket where basketball games are won and lost. "In the paint," Malone says, "either put up or shut up. It's where men are made. If you're a boy, you should be home with your mom." Colorful, yes, but it's not always pretty.

When you are six foot nine (206 cm), 256 pounds (116 kg), with not-to-be-believed biceps and a svelte thirty-one-inch (79-cm) waist, you are entitled to your opinion. These days, Malone is the living, breathing definition of basketball's power forward. To call him prototypical is almost unfair. No one may ever match his combination of speed and power.

As Golden State Warriors coach Don Nelson says, "He runs the court like a small man, then overpowers bigger people."

As the name implies, the power forward is generally smaller than the center and more agile. He plays farther from the basket but is expected to provide both scoring and rebounding with muscle and a quick burst of acceleration. He is basketball's equivalent to a linebacker, both physically and mentally. Unlike centers, power forwards are not permitted to lumber back on defense when a fast break is in progress. Unlike finesse forwards, there is more than just scoring in the job description. If there is dirty work to be done, the power forward is expected to do it: Scoring. Rebounds. Defense. Blocked shots. Steals.

Malone takes umbrage at the accepted terminology. "I'm a hard forward," he says. "You are either a forward or you aren't. I don't see how these guys let people call them small forwards. That's an insult."

Malone has it all, including a great nickname. In college, a Louisiana sportswriter dubbed him "The Mailman" because he always delivered in the games he played. Like many NBA stars, Malone began slowly and gathered speed as he learned his own strength, and in his case, this was at Louisiana Tech.

In three seasons there, Malone averaged 18.7 points and 9.3 rebounds per game. Although he had a year of eligibility left, Malone entered the 1985 draft. The NBA was not terribly impressed. Malone was the thirteenth player taken in the first round, but he placed third in Rookie of the Year balloting after his initial season. Malone averaged 14.9 points and 8.9 rebounds per game and his confidence grew as the season progressed. He was the leading playoff scorer (21.8 points per game) for the Jazz.

Malone's regular-season scoring average climbed sharply to 21.7 in 1986–87, to 27.7 in 1987–88, to 29.1 in 1988–89, and to 31.0 in 1989–90. In his fifth professional season, Malone evolved into one of the league's bona fide superstars. He became the ninth NBA player to average more than thirty points and ten rebounds per game. Center Moses Malone had been the last to do it, in 1981–82. Karl Malone led the Jazz in scoring in seventy-three of eighty-two games and threw in a career-high sixty-one points against Milwaukee on January 27, 1990. His 2,540 points eclipsed Adrian Dantley's previous record of 2,457. At the same time, Malone was one of the league's toughest defenders. For all these reasons, he was fourth in the balloting for the 1990 MVP. Oddly enough, Malone wasn't first among power forwards. Philadelphia 76ers' Charles Barkley placed second overall, just behind Los Angeles Lakers point guard Magic Johnson. Barkley, in fact, received more first-place votes than anyone. This was more a testament to the 76ers' lack of depth than any performance advantage over Malone.

Barkley, at six foot six (198 cm), 252 pounds (114 kg), is hardly the sculpted stuff of Malone, but his athletic ability and intensity are unquestioned. For his size, Barkley is astonishingly quick. He can (and does) dribble behind the back on his dazzling coast-to-coast plays and his hands are terrific. In the first six seasons of his career, Barkley averaged 1.6 steals and 3.7 assists per game. That's just a bonus, though. His mentality is perfectly suited to the position; if Barkley were a dog, he'd be a Doberman pinscher. The ugly business of power forward is what Barkley does best. Maybe it goes back to getting cut from the 1984 U.S. Olympic team by coach Bobby Knight. The U.S. won the gold medal easily, with perhaps the best amateur basketball team ever assembled, but it didn't include Barkley. "The Olympic thing really didn't bother me

© Brian Drake/Allsport

Through rain, ice, and snow "The Mailman" always delivers. Karl Malone of the Utah Jazz is the consummate power forward.

that much," Barkley says today. "For me, it's always been a matter of personal pride. I do it for pride, not for friends or family or the money. Just for the pride. Just for myself."

Chicago power forward Horace Grant was victimized for thirty-four points and twenty rebounds by Barkley in the third game of their 1990 playoff series. "When the refs let him play, he's impossible," Grant explained. "His favorite move is to stay in the lane for, like, about six seconds. Then, when the ball goes up, he grabs here [around the hips], gives me a yank, and pulls me behind him. Great move."

Earlier in the series, Barkley had lost some of his zest for the game in the face of Chicago's tireless double-team. Both Grant and Scottie Pippen forced Barkley to pass the ball out

to the perimeter, preventing him from charging directly at the basket. In the third game, Barkley posted up closer to the basket and left a trail of Bulls bodies in his wake. This is Barkley's modus operandi.

In Barkley's near-MVP season of 1989–90, he averaged 25.2 points and 11.5 rebounds per game. "It's becoming a cliché to say that Charles had a great season," said 76ers coach Jim Lynam. "Although his scoring average has dipped slightly, his all-around game keeps getting better. The leadership, intensity, and will to win make the team much more competitive."

At that point, Barkley had led the 76ers in scoring four straight seasons, rebounding (five), minutes played (three), and steals (two). It was just what Philadelphia envisioned when it drafted him fifth overall out of Auburn in 1984. Heading into the 1990–91 season, Barkley had compiled the third best shooting percentage in history (58.1), behind Artis Gilmore and James Donaldson. Barkley achieved his dream when the 76ers traded him to the Phoenix Suns in time for the 1992–93 season. Barkley promptly put together the season of his life, averaging 25.6 points and 12.2 rebounds per game. He was named the league's Most Valuable Player.

Among today's power forwards, Malone and Barkley are without peer. That's because Elvin Hayes played in the 1970s. At six foot nine (206 cm), he was the first of the modern power forwards. In his rookie season of 1969, Hayes led the NBA in scoring, compiling a 28.4 point average for the San Diego Rockets. In 1970 and 1974, Hayes, for the Capital Bullets, led the league in rebounding. Hayes called his place of work the "butcher shop," "because that's what it's like when people are trying to get a rebound. Every time a shot is taken there are going to be hips and elbows and chests and heads flying around, slamming and bumping. It's a rough proposition, one of the roughest you will find anywhere in sports."

A handful of NBA players are up for this grim task these days. Buck Williams of the Portland Trail Blazers is one of them. His work ethic is above reproach. Ask him how he refined rebounding to an art and he shrugs. "It's all about wanting to do it," Williams says. "I know it sounds simple, but that's what it comes down to."

Williams, six foot eight (203-cm) and 225 pounds (102-kg), came into the NBA in 1981–82 out of the University of Maryland and promptly threw up Rookie of the Year numbers. He ripped down 1,005 rebounds, an average of 12.3 per game, and managed 15.5 points each time out for the New Jersey Nets. Williams was an efficient, if reluctant, shooter; his career shooting percentage hovers around 55. But under the basket he was a terror. Williams reached the one-thousand rebound mark five times in his first six seasons and was named to the All-Star Game three times. Game in and game out, Williams did everything he could to win. The trouble was, the Nets couldn't assemble a worthy cast around him. Finally, in 1989, they set him free. He went to the Trail Blazers in exchange for Sam Bowie and a 1989 first-round draft choice.

Portland already had a terrific nucleus, with Clyde Drexler, Terry Porter, Kevin Duckworth, and Jerome Kersey, and Williams added the final ingredient: leadership. "He was on a team that at the end of the year was going nowhere," coach Rick Adelman says. "And he played like it was the first of the year." Soon, Portland was playing with new intensity.

At the age of thirty, Williams averaged 13.6 points and 9.8 rebounds per game, but those numbers don't tell the full story. Night after night, Williams guarded the toughest opposition scorers. At season's end, the Trail Blazers had shaved a full five points off their nightly allowance and Williams landed on the NBA's All-Defensive first team for the first time in his career. If Portland wins a league title in the early 1990s, Williams will have a large hand in it.

The Boston Celtics hoisted three championship banners at Boston Garden after Larry Bird arrived in 1979. But none of them came without the added presence of Kevin McHale in 1980. Trying to categorize Bird and McHale is difficult; in some respects, McHale is more of a finesse player around the basket and Bird, at times, applied muscle to his infinite moves. Still, McHale, at six foot ten (208 cm), 225 pounds (102 kg), generally guards the opponent's power forward.

He was the third player taken in the 1980 draft, from the University of Minnesota, and he gradually justified the choice. In the mid-1980s, McHale became a devastating weapon at both ends of the court. He evolved slowly, developing a variety of nifty moves around the basket. His scoring average increased in each of his first five seasons, and in 1985–86, it cracked the twenty-point barrier. Over two seasons, 1986–87 and 1987–88, McHale shot over 60 percent from the field. In 1986–87, McHale became the first player in league history to shoot better than 60 percent from the field and 80 percent from the free-throw line. Going into the 1991–92 season, McHale had the fourth-best shooting percentage in league history (56.2). While opponents were giving Bird special attention on defense, McHale was the Celtics' leading scorer in the 1985 and 1986 NBA championship series. At the same time, his long arms and formidable presence around the basket made life difficult for opposing shooters. McHale was named to the NBA's All-Defensive first team for three consecutive years, from 1986–88. In 1990–91, he was named to his seventh All-Star Game.

When young, marketable power forwards come up in trade talks, Charles Oakley's name is usually mentioned first. At six

Power forward is the ugliest of positions, as personified by the bruising strength of the Phoenix Suns' Charles Barkley, the National Basketball Association's Most Valuable Player for 1992–93.

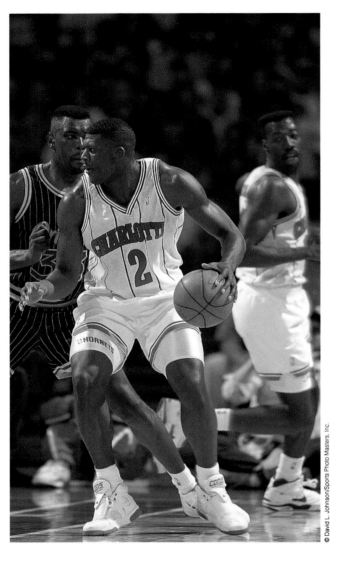

Atlantic Division title with Oakley doing his usual damage. Like Malone, Barkley, Williams, and McHale, Oakley's home is in the paint. And make no mistake, a night playing against those players in the paint is a brush with greatness.

# THE CENTER (5)

There was a time, 1944 to be precise, when center was officially recognized as basketball's dominant position. That was when the NCAA was forced to react to the presence of a six-foot-ten (208-cm) DePaul University center named George Mikan. He swatted away so many shots as they approached the net that the goaltending rule was introduced in time for his junior season. No matter. Mikan was still a force, intimidating opponents and altering shots. He also averaged twenty-three points a game his last two seasons at DePaul. Mikan became basketball's first dominant big man. He held court with the Minneapolis Lakers, and from 1948 to 1954, he was virtually unstoppable on both ends of the floor.

Previously, the center was simply the tallest player on the team, which sometimes left an only six-foot (183-cm) athlete in the pivot. The center was positioned in the center of the floor, close to the basket. Since centers weren't the most agile players, this worked on the offensive end because it shortened the shot to the basket. The defensive idea—Mikan's goaltending efforts notwithstanding—was to provide a last line of defense with long arms that changed shots and passes, however modestly.

In the late 1950s, two great centers arrived on the NBA scene who dominated everyone except each other. Bill Russell, six foot ten (208 cm) and 220 pounds (100 kg), left two NCAA titles in his wake at the University of San Francisco and joined the Boston Celtics in 1957. Wilt Chamberlain, perhaps the strongest man ever to play professional basketball, made his initial mark at the University of Kansas and then played one season with the Harlem Globetrotters. In 1959, he signed with the Philadelphia 76ers. Together, at opposite ends of the court, Russell and Chamberlain radically changed the center position.

Russell was arguably the most revolutionary figure in the history of basketball. His defensive style was the model for

foot nine (206 cm) and 245 pounds (111 kg), Oakley is good for an automatic eleven rebounds and thirteen points per game. He once toiled in the relative obscurity of Virginia Union University, where he averaged seventeen rebounds and twenty-four points per game. Those numbers came down in three seasons in Chicago, but that had more to do with Oakley's competition, rather than his waning intensity. He was absolutely relentless; in one memorable game, he pulled down thirty-five rebounds.

When Oakley arrived in New York in 1988 as part of the trade for center Bill Cartwright, he immediately complemented center Patrick Ewing. The Knicks went on to win the

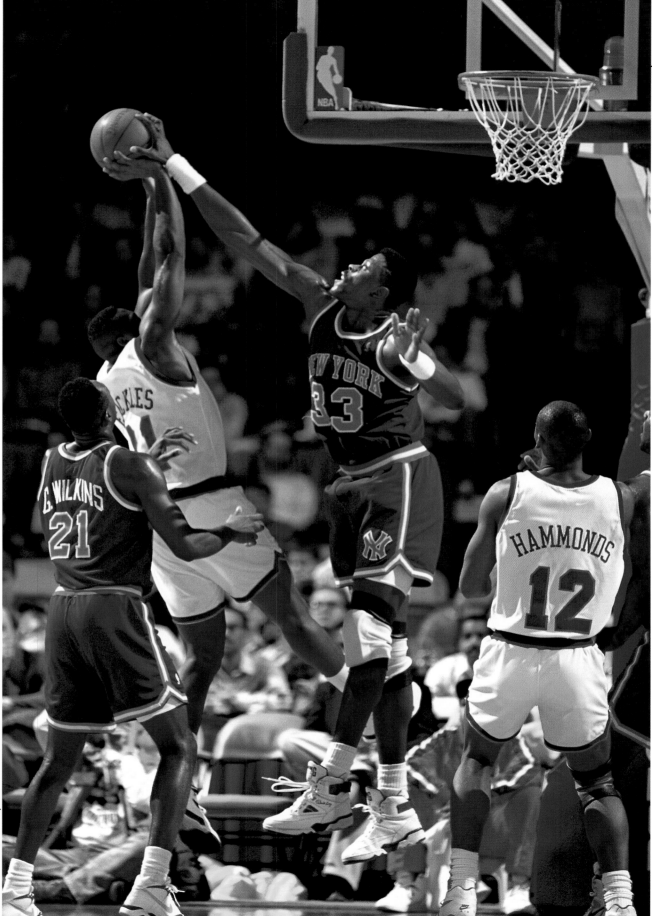

**Patrick Ewing of the New York Knicks worked on sharpening his skills and made himself a complete center.**

the contemporary center and in some ways spurred the departure from Mikan's plodding era and the evolution of the fast-paced game that has made the NBA so popular. Size was no longer a guarantee of dominance; creativity and agility were now necessary. Russell was not a scorer; rather, he placed a premium on shot-blocking and rebounding. His timing was extraordinary, and Russell could consistently steer a rejection in the direction of a teammate or make the outlet pass to start a fast break the other way. With Russell in the middle, the Boston Celtics won eleven NBA championships in a span of thirteen years.

"Basketball," Russell said, "is a game that involves a great deal of psychology. The psychology in defense is not blocking a shot or stealing a pass or getting the ball away. The psychology is to make the offensive team deviate from their normal habits. What I try to do on defense is make the offensive man do not what he wants to do, but what I want. I might block only five shots a game, but I'm the only one who knows which five."

Red Auerbach, Russell's coach in Boston, said in 1963, "Russell has had the biggest impact on the game in the last ten years because he introduced a new defensive weapon, the blocked shot. He has popularized the weapon to combat the aggressive, running-type game."

Russell was the essence of the intimidating defensive presence the center once had in basketball. Wilt Chamberlain, on the other hand, was terrifying when the ball was in his massive hands. At seven foot one (216 cm) and 275 pounds (125 kg), he was almost unstoppable moving toward the basket. The sight of the Big Dipper playing against mortals a foot shorter sometimes approached the comical; it seemed too easy. Chamberlain averaged 37.6 points per game his rookie season and became the first NBA player to win both the Rookie of the Year and Most Valuable Player awards in his first season. On March 2, 1962, Chamberlain ripped through the New York Knicks for an even 100 points. This was a feat similar to Bob Beamon's world-record high jump in the 1968 Olympic Games at Mexico City. It advanced the standard almost too far to comprehend. The previous NBA high was Elgin Baylor's seventy-one in 1960. Chamberlain averaged 50.4 points that year, an astounding figure. Still, his size and his hubris left people cold. "Nobody," he once said, "roots for Goliath."

Basketball's fourth most dominant center was Kareem Abdul-Jabbar. Growing up as Lew Alcindor in New York City, he watched Russell play against the Knicks in the 1960s at Madison Square Garden. He appreciated Russell's defense and team play, but Alcindor had another weapon in his repertoire: offense. The seven-foot-two (218-cm), 267-pound (121-kg) athlete averaged 26.4 points per game in four seasons at UCLA, along with 15.5 rebounds. The Bruins won three NCAA national titles, and his game continued to evolve in the professional ranks. He was the prototypical center; in some ways, he combined the best of Russell and Chamberlain. It is possible that there has never been a larger, more graceful athlete in the history of sport.

**Orlando's Shaquille O'Neal was the National Basketball Association's best rookie in 1992–93, averaging 23.4 points and 13.9 rebounds per game.**

© Noren Trotman/ Sports Photo Masters, Inc.

"I think I basically played for an idea, which is how close I could come to being my best," Abdul-Jabbar said. "I put some hard work into that. I had the good fortune to have been given talent, and I was lucky enough not to have gotten hurt."

Abdul-Jabbar dominated basketball longer than anyone before or after. He played for four years in college and another twenty for the Milwaukee Bucks and Los Angeles Lakers. In the twenty years he played professional ball, Abdul-Jabbar's teams won nine championships. When he retired after the 1989 season, suddenly, for the first time in forty years, there was no dominant center in basketball.

Today, despite the emergence of such talents as the San Antonio Spurs' David Robinson, the Houston Rockets' Hakeem Olajuwon, and the New York Knicks' Patrick Ewing, the center is no longer the center of the basketball universe. Blame the self-indulgent me-generation.

"Kids today love to play facing the basket," says Golden State Warriors coach Don Nelson. "The kids with skill want to play forward now. For whatever reason, the multipurpose, multitalented center doesn't exist in the college ranks. I think it's just a demise in the talent of big players."

Actually, there's more to it than that. For starters, the gritty, back-to-the-basket job description of center holds little appeal to the video generation. They want to score. The nature of the game has also changed in the last two decades. In an earlier era, power forwards like Karl Malone and Charles Oakley would have been centers. At six foot nine (206 cm) and close to 250 pounds (113 kg), they rotate on their own axes. Instead of playing on the wing like forwards of the past, they take the ball to the basket with passion and power. Defensively, they are more than capable of helping their own center under the basket. And so, being a center these days isn't as easy as it once was.

Ralph Sampson won't disagree. At seven foot four (223 cm), he was one of the most dominant centers in college basketball history. When his Virginia team played Patrick Ewing's Georgetown Hoyas in December 1982, it was a classic battle of big men. Sampson prevailed, producing twenty-three points, sixteen rebounds, and seven blocked shots. Ewing, whose Hoyas lost the larger battle, 68–63, could only counter with sixteen points, eight rebounds, and five blocked shots. Although his professional debut was similarly emphatic (Samp-

© Noren Trotman/ Sports Photo Masters, Inc.

son scored twenty points and pulled down fifteen rebounds for the Houston Rockets), he never realized his enormous promise. At 230 pounds (104 kg), he wasn't equipped to muscle opposing centers in the paint. Injuries and a perceived lack of aggressiveness held him back. After five productive seasons in Houston, Sampson faded from view. He played for three different teams in three years as little more than a high-priced, low-production finesse forward.

Is there no hope for a dominant center today? "Maybe Robinson will be the one," says Willis Reed, New York Knicks Hall of Fame center. "He's certainly the only guy with a realistic chance. Besides him, it's very slim pickings. If I was playing on

**David Robinson is a physical marvel. After serving a hitch in the Navy, he overpowered virtually every NBA center he faced.**

**Previous page: Kareem Abdul-Jabbar perfected the unstoppable shot, the Skyhook. It was so lethal that when he retired, Abdul-Jabbar had scored more professional points than anyone.**

the same team with Robinson I would probably be his backup or a power forward. There is no way I could play ahead of him. He has tremendous quickness and great lateral movement. His timing is unbelievable and he can shoot the ball."

Although Olajuwon had better scoring, rebounding, and blocked shots figures than Robinson in his rookie season of 1989–90, Robinson appears to be the genuine article. He is seven feet and one inch (216 cm) and 235 pounds (107 kg) of athlete. In his senior season at the Naval Academy, Robinson became the first player in NCAA Division I history to score more than 2,500 points, snare more than 1,300 rebounds, and

shoot more than 60 percent from the field. His 28.2 points per game were third in the nation, while his shot-blocking (4.5) and rebounding (11.8) averages were first and fourth, respectively. As a junior, Robinson set an NCAA record by blocking fourteen shots on January 4, 1986, against North Carolina-Wilmington. Five nights later, he rejected twelve James Madison shots, tying the second-highest total ever.

Aware that Robinson had to serve two years in the military before joining the team, the Spurs nevertheless made him the first overall draft choice in 1987, signed him to an eight-year, $26 million contract, and then waited patiently for their sav-

Hakeem Olajuwon came to basketball and is still improving as he approaches his thirties. Olajuwon has amazing quickness for his size, as his steals totals attest.

ior. When he entered the league for the 1989–90 season, critics wondered if Robinson, with a thirty-three-inch (84-cm) waist, was strong enough to survive with the big boys.

"I was clotheslined and elbowed," Robinson said. "But that's the league. You know it's coming and it's a great challenge. Until a few years ago, I was pretty obscure. I feel like I'm talented, but I'm just starting to grow."

In 1988–89, the Spurs' record was 21–61. A year later, with Robinson in the lineup, San Antonio was 56–26, achieving the largest single-season turnaround in NBA history. He was far and away the league's Rookie of the Year, posting a scoring average of 24.3 points, 12.0 rebounds, and 3.9 blocked shots. His quickness also allowed him 257 steals, more than a few resulting from a hustle down the court to strip guards in a fast-break transition. In his first four seasons playing for San Antonio, Robinson averaged 24.2 points and 12.2 rebounds per game.

Robinson plays with his back to the basket in the classic style. He backs his man down to the basket, spins, and muscles his way to the hoop. He has other options as well: He has a soft turnaround jump shot off glass and a brutal one-handed slam dunk. And he can run the floor. Since he is left-handed, Robinson is especially difficult to defend, since most centers are used to right-handed opponents. As a rookie, concentration was his only problem. As San Antonio coach Larry Brown says, there is room for improvement. "He had a terrific year, but I think he's going to have to develop a go-to shot," says Brown, perhaps thinking of Abdul-Jabbar's Skyhook. "We were thrilled with his performance, but there is no doubt in my mind that he can get better. He will develop a shot, and he will learn to play harder more often. He's an intelligent guy, and I think because of that, and because he played a year, he will get better. I really think that because David sat out two years it hurt him. Everyone says it helped him mature, but he didn't get to play a lot of basketball in that time."

Robinson, who played only one year of high school basketball, had played only six seasons of organized ball when the 1990–91 NBA season began. His potential is frightening. "He's the closest thing to [Bill] Russell I've ever seen with that kind of speed and ability to play defense," says Celtics Hall of Famer Bob Cousy, who was on the receiving end of many Russell outlet passes.

© J. Giamundo/B. Bennett Studios

If attitude means anything, Robinson has an opportunity to dominate the game as few before him have. "I don't like to lose at anything," he says. "I don't want to say it's pride in yourself, because I think that word is overused, but it's being able to feel good about yourself. When I was a kid, I did a lot of different things. I tried hard to find something I was really great at. So when I grew to be six foot eight [203 cm] in high school and I started developing as a basketball player, I told myself, 'This is your thing. This is the thing to go after.' Basketball is my chance to be great."

Until Robinson realizes that potential, which seems imminent, Hakeem Olajuwon offers the biggest presence in the pivot. Like Robinson, Olajuwon came relatively late to the game and continues to improve each year. In 1989–90, the Rockets' six-foot-ten (208 cm), 250-pound (113 kg) center averaged 24.3 points per game, to go with 14.0 rebounds and 4.59 blocked shots. The latter two figures led the NBA, making Olajuwon the first player since Bill Walton (1976–77) to win those titles. In 1988–89, Olajuwon became the first player in league history to surpass two hundred blocks and two hundred steals. In a sense, Olajuwon is still discovering his capabilities. Before the 1990–91 season, he lifted weights and did some distance and speed running. He thinks better numbers are possible.

"That is the way I feel," he says. "I have tried to get in mid-season shape, and I feel good about it. I have six years' experience, I have the physique. I am ready to just have fun."

Amazingly, Olajuwon did not begin playing basketball until the age of seventeen. He was born in Lagos, Nigeria, and grew up playing handball. In 1978, when Muslim Teachers College in Lagos found itself in the All-Nigeria Teachers Sports Festival

in Sokoto, Olajuwon was drafted to the basketball team. Two years later he enrolled at the University of Houston. The Cougars went 88–16 in his three seasons there. Olajuwon became the eighth center in history to lead his team to the NCAA Final Four in three consecutive seasons. Houston lost all three times, but the Rockets had seen enough to draft Olajuwon in the first round. After six seasons, he has a piece of seventeen franchise records and four league marks, including the most seasons (three) finishing in the top ten in four different categories: scoring, rebounding, blocked shots, and steals.

The Knicks' Patrick Ewing has been Olajuwon's rival at center since he entered the NBA, burdened by expectation, in

**Everywhere he's played, Moses Malone has been the center of the universe. Through fifteen seasons, he had scored more than 25,000 points.**

**The Detroit Pistons' Bill Laimbeer isn't particularly swift or powerful, but he always seems to be around the action.**

1985. At seven feet (213 cm) and 240 pounds (109 kg), Ewing dominated his games at Georgetown University, where the Hoyas won the 1984 NCAA title. Coached by John Thompson, Ewing was more comfortable at the defensive end of the court. While Ewing averaged 9.2 rebounds per game, his scoring average was a modest 15.3 in four seasons at Georgetown.

When the Knicks made him the first pick in the 1985 draft, secure with a ten-year, $30 million contract, Ewing began to hone his offensive game. He learned how to free himself for the turnaround jump shot and how to release a soft hook shot from eight feet (2.4 m) away. He averaged an even twenty points his rookie season, but his defense and his intensity were found wanting. Four years later, Ewing broke through with the monster season that people had been predicting for him. He scored a Knicks record 2,347 points, for an average of 28.6 per game. Ewing set another team mark with 327 blocked shots (3.98) and averaged 10.9 rebounds. He was among the NBA's top six in scoring, rebounds, blocked shots, and shooting percentage. Ewing, who had noticeably sharpened his passing skills as well, made himself a complete center. What is left for him?

"I'm greedy," Ewing says. "I really don't have much to point to in terms of achievements in the league. But I want to win several championships and I want to win the MVP award. No choices. I want both."

Other centers of note: Boston's ageless Robert Parrish continued to be remarkably productive in the 1990–91 season at the age of thirty-seven, making the All-Star Game for the ninth time in fifteen seasons. Detroit's Bill Laimbeer functions well as center of the Pistons' championship team. Utah's Mark Eaton became more than a seven-foot-four (223-cm), 290-pound (131-kg) curiosity. He blocked 201 shots in 1989–90 to become the second-leading shot-blocker in NBA history (2,592) behind Abdul-Jabbar. Moreover, Eaton's size allowed the four other Jazz players the freedom to play one-on-one defense. The Utah scheme is to funnel offensive players into the middle, where Eaton's enormous wingspan is a serious threat, evoking shades of George Mikan.

After a rough rookie season, Ron Seikaly of the Miami Heat shows promise. In 1989–90, he averaged 16.6 points and 10.4 rebounds per game and was named the league's Most Improved Player.

It's almost not fair when seven-foot-four center Mark Eaton goes up to block a shot for the Utah Jazz. Here, Xavier McDaniel feels the shadow of Eaton's reach.

The rattle and hum of professional basketball is like nothing else: From the raw power of the New York Knicks' Charles Oakley, (inset), to the muscular struggle between Scottie Pippen of the Chicago Bulls and the Detroit Pistons' Dennis Rodman.

## CHAPTER THREE

# THE PRO GAME

1

5

4

© Wide World Photos, Inc.

2

**Shawn Bradley was an intimidating force in the middle for Brigham Young University, but the 90-inch question is: Can he dominate for the Philadelphia 76ers in the National Basketball Association?**

He wasn't particularly pretty to look at, but George Mikan was remarkably agile for his eighty-two inches. After Mikan, big was considered better in the NBA.

# THE GREAT PROFESSIONAL PLAYERS

Professional basketball has always been different from the college game. These days, NBA rookies are signed to multimillion-dollar contracts and most spend considerable time on the bench. However, considering exhibition games, an eighty-two-game regular season, and playoff games, a first-year professional can conceivably play nearly as many games in his debut season as in his four years of college.

There are rare players, like Boston Celtics center Bill Russell, who make the transition from college to professional ball seamlessly. Russell led the University of San Francisco to the NCAA title in 1956 and carried the Celtics to the NBA title in 1957. In between, he won a gold medal as a member of the U.S. Olympic team. With Russell as a pillar in the middle, the Celtics won eleven championship banners in thirteen seasons. Clearly, his performance at the professional level outstripped his contribution to the college game.

Below are ten players, profiled in chronological order, who helped carry the professional game to a new level.

(Guard Oscar Robertson had a magnificent professional career, and like Russell, he appeared in twelve All-Star Games, but Robertson was positively dominant in college, where he led all NCAA Division I players in scoring for three years running at the University of Cincinnati. For that reason, you'll find Robertson's feats chronicled in the college section of great players, beginning on page 100.)

## George Mikan

The NBA individual record book is dotted with fine print that repeatedly features names like Chamberlain, Russell, Baylor, and West. It isn't very often that the name George Lawrence Mikan, Jr., arises. In terms of the game's evolution, however, Mikan's is a big name, indeed. At six foot ten (208 cm) and 245 pounds (111 kg), Mikan changed the way the game would be played forever. When the Associated Press began a quest for the greatest basketball player of the first half of the twentieth century, this national wire service ultimately settled on Mikan. And why not?

He was born on June 18, 1924, in Joliet, Illinois, and played

© Naismith Memorial Basketball Hall of Fame

high school basketball at Chicago's Quigley Prep. Mikan was reasonably agile, considering his bulk, and developed an accurate short-range shot. His glasses belied a ferocious competitor's hunger for the ball. He was named College Player of the Year in 1945 and 1946 when he played for coach Ray Meyer at DePaul University and led the nation in scoring with a 23.2-point scoring average. DePaul won the NIT in 1945, and Mikan set ten individual records, including an eye-opening fifty-three point game.

Mikan's first professional season, 1946–47, was with the Chicago American Gears of the National Basketball League (NBL). Mikan averaged 16.5 points per game, and the Gears won the NBL championship. After the Chicago franchise folded, Mikan was awarded to the Minneapolis Lakers. Mikan averaged 21.3 points per game, and not coincidentally, the Lakers won the NBL title in 1948. When Minneapolis joined the NBA for the 1948–49 season, Mikan immediately dominated the league. He averaged 28.3 points per game to lead the NBA in scoring; only two other players, Joe Fulks of Philadelphia and Chicago's Max Zaslofsky, averaged more than twenty. The Lakers finished a game behind Rochester in the

Western Division over the regular season, but swept past both Chicago and Rochester in the playoffs to set up a meeting with Washington in the finals. The Lakers prevailed in six games, winning the championship. With Mikan in the middle, Minneapolis won the title five times in six seasons. Including that NIT crown, Mikan won championships in eight of ten seasons.

Being the obvious big man, the acknowledged front-runner, gave opponents more reason than ever to try to beat Mikan and the Lakers, but it also fueled Mikan's gritty resolve. "It was constantly a test as to whether or not I was able to beat the other guy," Mikan says. "It was a day-to-day type of competition. Every time I played, they wanted to beat me. But being stubborn and determined, I wouldn't let them."

Mikan, who was elected to the Basketball Hall of Fame in 1959, served as the first commissioner of the ABA, which spawned such greats as Julius Erving and Rick Barry.

## Bob Cousy

While many of the "giants" of the early professional game were just that, the diminutive Bob Cousy stood apart. Although he gave away nearly ten inches (25 cm) and some seventy pounds (34 kg) to Mikan, Cousy was similarly influential, but in a different way. Robert J. Cousy, born August 9, 1928, in New York City, did it with dazzle. He could shoot well enough, but it was his passing that thrilled people. Just as Arnold Palmer helped push golf over the top in the public consciousness, the charismatic Cousy is credited with focusing national attention on professional basketball in the critical decade of the 1950s.

After a career at Andrew Jackson High School in Queens, Cousy attended Holy Cross College, where the team won the NCAA title in 1947. He did not come by his skills easily; Cousy spent an entire college summer working on his celebrated behind-the-back pass. But would Cousy's game play in the NBA? The Boston Celtics didn't think so, at least not initially. They passed on Cousy in the draft, selecting seven-foot (213-cm) Charlie Share of Bowling Green. Cousy went to the Tri-City Hawks, who traded him to the Chicago Stags for Gene Vance. When the franchise went under a few months later,

Cousy's name was thrown into a hat, literally, and pulled out by Boston owner Walter Brown.

Cousy, dubbed "Houdini of the Hardwoods," brought a spectacular balance to the Celtics. As the point guard, Cousy controlled virtually every element of the game. In 1952–53, his third season, Cousy led the league with 7.7 assists per game and was third in scoring, with a 19.8 point average. Cousy had terrific peripheral vision on the court; he seemed to spot open teammates with the back of his head. As the Celtics improved, attendance swelled from an average of 3,608 fans in 1946–47 to the league record of 10,517 who watched the Celtics win their first NBA title in 1957. Beyond his pure statistics, Cousy was one of the great clutch performers in NBA history. In a memorable quadruple-overtime playoff victory over Syracuse in 1953, Cousy scored fifty points, breaking Mikan's record of forty-seven. Cousy was a scintillating thirty-for-thirty-two from the foul line. At one point in overtime, Cousy drilled eighteen straight free throws. Cousy was personally responsible for rallying the Celtics from a seventeen-point deficit in the seventh game of the division finals against Syracuse in 1959. After that, Boston swept Minneapolis in the championship final.

Cousy led the NBA in assists eight straight seasons and finished his career with 6,955 passes for baskets and 16,960 points. He appeared in thirteen All-Star Games, one for each season he played in the league. They called him "Mr. Basketball," and without his spectacular style, the game might not have caught fire the way it did.

## Bob Pettit

One name that should be included in any study of professional basketball's formative years is Robert Lee Pettit, Jr. He wasn't the tallest, the quickest, or the slickest on the court, but he was six foot nine (206 cm), 215 pounds (97 kg), and could shoot and rebound with skill to match. Consider the statistical wreckage Pettit left behind him when he retired from the NBA after eleven seasons: He was first in all-time scoring, with 20,880 points, fifth in scoring average (26.4 points), and third in rebounding, with 12,849 boards. He dominated the game at his position every bit as much as Elvin

Hayes did in his era. And yet, today the contributions of the St. Louis Hawks' forward are often overlooked.

That he could score at will and still worked hard at both ends to secure rebounds underlined the intensity that Pettit brought to each game. He developed his work ethic playing high school basketball in Baton Rouge, Louisiana, where he was born on December 12, 1932. He graduated to the local college, Louisiana State University, where he averaged a blazing 27.4 points per game. His stats showed little drop-off at the professional level.

Pettit averaged 20.4 points in his rookie season in Milwaukee, 1954–55, and was selected to play in the All-Star Game. He would be named to the All-NBA First Team for the next decade. When the franchise moved to St. Louis the following season, Pettit really caught fire. His scoring and rebounding averages soared to 25.7 points and 16.2, respectively. Only Clyde Lovellette of Minneapolis (21.5 points and

14.0 rebounds), Syracuse's Dolph Schayes (20.4 points and 12.4 rebounds), and Neil Johnston of Philadelphia (22.1 points and 12.5 rebounds) were even in the same league. Pettit earned the MVP award at the All-Star Game and received it again after his great second season. For nine consecutive seasons, Pettit maintained those numbers.

Not fortunate enough to be surrounded by championship-caliber players like Boston's Bob Cousy, for a brief, shining moment Pettit carried the Hawks past the mighty Celtics. The two teams advanced to the finals in the 1957–58 season and split the first four games, with the visiting team winning each time. On April 9, 1958, the Hawks squeezed past the Celtics 102–100 at Boston Garden. Three days later, back in St. Louis, Pettit single-handedly held off a Boston charge. He scored nineteen of the Hawks' final twenty-one points and finished with fifty as the Hawks won their first and only NBA championship with a 110–109 victory.

**The Boston Celtics' Bill Russell brought tenacious rebounding and defense to the table like no one before or after.**

# Bill Russell

The Hawks' title was well-deserved, but there was one qualifier in their surprising win over the Celtics. Center William Felton Russell had gone down with an injury in Game Three of the championship series. In the Celtics' run of eight consecutive NBA titles, from 1959 to 1966, Russell clearly was the team's Most Valuable Player. His statistics didn't always show it since he was supported by flashier teammates like Bob Cousy, Bill Sharman, and Tommy Heinsohn. Russell's craft went beyond the simple art of scoring. Mining territory that was harder to appreciate, Russell, whose strengths were rebounding and shot-blocking, may have been the greatest defensive player ever. These were the skills that contributed the most to the Celtics' eleven championship banners in his thirteen seasons in Boston.

No one saw it coming. Russell was born on February 12, 1934, in Monroe, Louisiana, and though he was extraordinarily tall at an early age, his prowess on the court did not mark him for great things. At McClymonds High School in Oakland, California, Russell shared the junior varsity's fifteenth jersey with teammate Roland Campbell as a sophomore. Russell finally made the varsity team as a six-foot-four (193-cm) junior, but played little. As a senior starter, his best game was a fourteen-point effort. What he lacked on the offensive end, Russell made up for with determination on defense. At the University of San Francisco, he developed the extraordinary timing and reflexes that would one day alter the way the game was played.

In the Mikan Era, the ball was rebounded and pushed methodically up the floor. Russell learned to swat his rejected shots in the direction of his teammates, which started them off the other way. When he rebounded the ball, Russell would throw a quick outlet pass that led to a fast break. And so it became recognized that an agile defender in the middle could catalyze the running game.

The University of San Francisco Dons won fifty-five straight games with Russell, now six foot ten (208 cm), in the lineup, including two NCAA titles. When Russell entered the NBA, his defense was a known quantity; the question was, could he produce on offense? Russell, the highest-paid rookie in league history, averaged a monstrous 19.6 rebounds per

game, but he also scored 14.7 points each time out. Lost in his numbing career rebounding numbers (a total of 21,620, second only to Wilt Chamberlain) is a serviceable scoring average of 15.1 points.

His overall impact was not lost on those who followed the game. Russell was named the league's MVP five times, in 1958, 1961, 1962, 1963, and 1965. In 1980, the Professional Basketball Writers of America confirmed what many believed all along; they named Russell the greatest player in the history of the NBA.

# Elgin Baylor

Bo Jackson, who doubled as a running back for the Los Angeles Raiders and a slugger for the Chicago White Sox, redefined the notion of the two-sport athlete. We know it is now possible to participate at the highest levels of professional athletics if the talent is there. Chances are, Elgin Gay Baylor could have pulled off the rare double if given the chance.

Born in Washington, D.C., on September 16, 1934, Baylor was recruited as a football receiver by the College of Idaho in 1954. Rain forced football practice inside one day and Baylor wound up in a pickup hoops game, twisting his formidable six-foot-five (196-cm), 225-pound (102-kg) body every which way around the basket. The basketball coach was mesmerized, and it wasn't long before Baylor, the football recruit, became Baylor, the basketball recruit. He averaged 31.3 points a game that season, before transferring to Seattle University. As a senior, Baylor averaged nineteen rebounds and thirty-one points per game.

The Lakers, still in Minneapolis at the time, selected him in the first round of the 1958 draft. Baylor averaged 24.9 points and 15 rebounds per game his first year, making him the obvious choice for the NBA Rookie of the Year. He played in an era when the best players rarely made over half of their shots. To achieve his riveting career average of 27.4 points per game and score 8,693 baskets, Baylor took a daunting 20,171 shots from the field—a success rate of 43.1 percent. But the number doesn't begin to describe Baylor's value to the Lakers.

When he was hot, nothing could stop him. He was fluid and smooth and possessed one of the game's prettiest shots. He was also deceptively powerful in sorties to the basket. Baylor scored seventy-one points in one playoff game against the New York Knicks in 1960, and in 1962, he scorched the Boston Celtics with sixty-one points in an important playoff game. The record stood for twenty-two years, until Michael Jordan caught fire for sixty-three points against the same Celtics. When Baylor left the game after the 1972 season, he had scored 23,149 points, the third highest total ever. His scoring average was surpassed only by Wilt Chamberlain and Oscar Robertson. Primarily a shooter, an overlooked area of Baylor's game was rebounding; he averaged a gaudy 13.5 boards per game over his career and finished as the league's fifth-leading rebounder.

# Wilt Chamberlain

He stood seven foot one (216 cm), weighed 275 pounds (125 kg), and was truly a giant among giants. Wilton N. Chamberlain was the most dominant offensive player in the history of basketball. Sure, Kareem Abdul-Jabbar scored more points, but he played for twenty seasons. Chamberlain produced 31,419 points in fourteen seasons and his average of 30.1 per game, the highest in history, is far ahead of Abdul-Jabbar's 24.6. And what can you say about a man who averages 50.4 points over an entire season, as Chamberlain did in 1962? Or scores 100 points in a single game, as Chamberlain did on March 2 of that epic season?

Chamberlain was born in Philadelphia on August 21, 1936, one of nine children. At the age of fifteen, Chamberlain was already six foot ten (208 cm). After a career at Overbrook High School, Chamberlain went on to the University of Kansas, where his legend began to grow. He averaged 29.9 points per game before joining the Harlem Globetrotters for the 1958–59 season. "Wilt the Stilt" played to the crowd as well as any of the traveling troupe, but his greatest challenges lay ahead in the NBA, where Russell and the skeptics awaited.

The two big men first met during the 1959–60 season and their classic confrontations helped professional basketball evolve. "That's what the league wanted to sell," says Bob Cousy, Russell's Celtics teammate. "In those days a big-name college player was used to sell tickets in just about every arena, but when Wilt came out it was something special. The interest was phenomenal."

Chamberlain tore up the NBA, averaging 37.6 points and 26.9 rebounds per game. He became the first player in league history with the dual distinction of being named Most Valuable Player and Rookie of the Year in the same season. Chamberlain's numbers were hard to comprehend. He seemed to move at will on the court, even when Russell and the Celtics were the opposition. Chamberlain led the league in scoring for seven consecutive seasons. In 1961–62, when he averaged 50.4 points per game, Chamberlain became the first NBA player to reach the 4,000 point mark, scoring an unheard of 4,029 points. He was the league's MVP four times, in 1960, 1966, 1967, and 1968. Moreover, he led all players in field goal percentage nine times. Chamberlain also led the league in rebounding eleven times. In 1967–68, Chamberlain handed out 702 assists to become the first center ever to lead the NBA in assists.

And although Chamberlain never accumulated the championship banners that Russell did, he was every bit his equal. As always, Chamberlain was larger than life.

# Jerry West

The great players want the ball at crunch time. In today's game, Michael Jordan of the Chicago Bulls takes over when his team needs him in the fourth quarter. In the playoffs, Jordan seems to find another gear. So it was with Jerry Alan West. They called him "Mr. Clutch," and until Michael Jordan came along, West's playoff scoring average of 29.1 points per game was the best in NBA history. Winning seemed to always follow in his wake.

West was born in Cheylan, West Virginia, on May 28, 1938, and carried East Bank High School (Virginia) to the 1956 state championship. West, who possessed one of the game's most accurate and aesthetic jumpshots, averaged thirty-two points per game and became the first schoolboy in state history to reach the nine-hundred-point plateau. He did the same thing at West Virginia University. West averaged 24.8 points over four seasons and led the Mountaineers to the NCAA finals in 1959. He was named the tournament's MVP. There were gold

© Manny Rubio

Beyond his epic size, Wilt Chamberlain brought a monstrous passion to the game. His record of 100 points in a single game remains one of the most untouchable records in all of sports.

**Los Angeles Lakers guard Jerry West, "Mr. Clutch," was the quintessential crunch-time performer.**

© Manny Rubio

All-Defensive Team selection four different times. In 1970, West led the league in scoring, with a 31.2 point average; two years later, he was the NBA's assist leader with 747.

Even at the advanced age of thirty-six, West remained a startlingly effective player. In his fourteenth and final season in Los Angeles, West averaged 22.8 points per game and managed a total of 607 assists. He graduated to become the coach of the Lakers in 1976 and compiled a 145–101 record over three seasons. In 1982, West was elevated to general manager. He had won only one NBA title as a player, but in a strange twist of fate, Los Angeles won three NBA titles in the first eight seasons of West's tenure.

# John Havlicek

He stood six foot five (196 cm) and weighed 205 pounds (93 kg), which even in the early 1960s, made him something players call a "tweener." John Havlicek was more than that; he was one of the best guard-forward swingmen in the history of the NBA. He had the quickness and vision to play guard, and the strength and the willpower to play forward. Most of all, he had the endurance to run up and down the court long after others took to the bench.

"My game has always been to go as hard as I can, as long as I can," Havlicek said midway through his sixteen-year professional career.

It was no idle boast. His teammates joked that doctors would line up to perform his autopsy, just to see what it was that made him tick. For a player who wasn't always a starter in his early career, Havlicek averaged a lot of playing time, some thirty-five minutes a game. In fact, Havlicek raised the position of sixth man to an art form. "No one," said Bill Russell, Havlicek's coach and teammate with the Boston Celtics, "can come off the bench and spark a team like John Havlicek."

Havlicek was born on April 8, 1940, in Martins Ferry, Ohio. At Bridgeport High School, Havlicek was a good basketball and baseball player, but football seemed to be his calling. He was an All-State quarterback on a .500 team, which bespeaks his ability. Ohio State football coach Woody Hayes liked him enough to offer him a scholarship, but he instead accepted a basketball scholarship to Ohio State. Havlicek joined fellow

medals at the Pan-American Games and, a year later, at the 1960 Olympics in Rome. That was the same year the Minneapolis Lakers chose him second overall in the draft and then moved west to Los Angeles.

It took the six-foot-two (188-cm), 185-pound (84-kg) guard a year to adjust to the NBA, but in the 1961–62 season, West emerged as one of the league's most polished players. He could score, as his average of 30.8 indicated, and he could do it under pressure. West was also a tenacious defensive player. He made the All-NBA First Team ten times, but he also was an

Ohio all-stars Larry Siegfried and Jerry Lucas as freshmen in 1958; all three became professional players. In their junior season, they led the Buckeyes to the 1960 NCAA championship. Havlicek's numbers for three collegiate seasons were hardly scintillating (14.6 points and 8.6 rebounds per game), but he was a well-rounded player who knew how to win.

Recognizing this, the Celtics offered him a professional contract, but again football complicated the issue. The Cleveland Browns drafted him as a wide receiver in the seventh round of the 1962 draft. Havlicek signed with Cleveland and played in an exhibition game against the Pittsburgh Steelers. That was all it took to convince Havlicek that roundball was his forte. For four years, Havlicek was Celtics coach Red Auerbach's first man off the bench. Finally, after the Celtics won three straight titles, Auerbach moved Havlicek into the starting lineup. He averaged 20.8 points and 4.8 rebounds per game and helped the Celtics win eight championship banners. Havlicek could do it all: score, rebound, pass, and shoot under pressure. His playoff scoring average (22.0) was better than his regular-season mark, and in 1974, he was the NBA Playoff MVP.

**John Havlicek of the Boston Celtics was a forerunner in more ways than one.**

© Manny Rubio

This page: Julius Erving, the good doctor, essentially coined the phrase "hang time." Opposite: The bottom line? No one played more NBA minutes than Kareem Abdul-Jabbar, and no one scored more points.

© D. Strohmeyer/Allsport

## Julius Erving

His name was Julius Winfield Erving II, but his teammates called him "Doc."

The name first surfaced at Roosevelt High School in New York. "In high school," Erving once explained, "a friend of mine kept telling me he was going to be a professor, so I told him I was going to be a doctor. We just started calling each other that, professor and doctor. And later on, in the Rucker League in Harlem when people started calling me 'Black Moses' and 'Houdini,' I told them if they wanted to call me anything, call me Doctor."

It is no exaggeration to say that Dr. J carried an entire league on his modest shoulders. He soared and swooped to the basket as no one before him, and his charisma helped keep the ABA afloat long enough to force the NBA to take in four of its teams. Erving may have been the player most responsible for elevating basketball from a horizontal to a vertical game. He was the first player with the ability to take off at the foul line, fifteen feet (4.6 m) from the basket, and slam-dunk the ball home.

Erving was born in Roosevelt, New York, on February 22, 1950, and wound up at the University of Massachusetts as a six-foot-seven (201-cm), 210-pound (95-kg) forward who could fly. He averaged more than twenty-six points a game for three seasons. By 1971, after he became the seventh player in collegiate history to average over twenty points and twenty rebounds per game in a career, it seemed that the college game was no longer a challenge for Erving. He signed as an undergraduate free agent with Virginia of the ABA and was spectacular in two seasons there. Erving broke in with a scoring average of 27.3 points per game and pushed it to 31.9 the following season to lead the fledgling league. In 1973, Virginia traded Erving to the New York Nets, where he blazed into national prominence with ceiling-scraping journeys to the basket at Nassau Coliseum. For three seasons with the Nets, Erving averaged more than twenty-eight points per game and earned at least a share of the ABA's MVP award each year.

It was inevitable that Erving would rise to a higher league. He entered the NBA with the Nets in 1976, but was promptly sold to the Philadelphia 76ers. In eleven seasons there, Erving averaged twenty-two points per game, made the All-Star Game all eleven years, and was the league's MVP in 1981. He earned his first and only NBA championship ring in 1983. Erving was ethereal in flight and was consistently effective as well. His 30,026 professional points are exceeded only by Wilt Chamberlain's 31,419 and Kareem Abdul-Jabbar's 38,387.

## Kareem Abdul-Jabbar

He stood seven foot two (218 cm), was powerful enough to slam-dunk the ball through the most nettlesome defense, and was agile and athletic enough to develop an unblockable piece of work called the Skyhook. He wasn't as strong as Chamberlain or as light on his feet as Julius Erving, but the thing Kareem Abdul-Jabbar did better than anyone in NBA history was endure. The record book belongs to him: most points scored (38,387), most games played (1,560), most minutes played (57,446), most field goals attempted (28,307), most field goals made (15,837), most blocked shots (3,189).

The quality and quantity of Abdul-Jabbar's career may never be matched. He was the first and, perhaps, the last player in NBA history to celebrate a silver anniversary (20 seasons). In that time, he won six NBA titles and became the

only player to win six league MVP awards. Everywhere he played, he was a winner.

He was born with the name Lew Alcindor in Harlem, New York, on April 16, 1947. He lived with his parents on 111th Street, a block from Central Park, and learned the game of basketball on the city's playground courts. As a freshman, he was the starting center for Power Memorial, an all-boys Catholic school in the heart of Manhattan. During his four-year tenure there, Power Memorial won ninety-five games, including a seventy-one-game winning streak, and lost six. At UCLA, he scored thirty-three points per game as a freshman, then led the Bruins to three NCAA championships. He was the Tournament MVP all three times. UCLA's record in those three seasons was a breathtaking 88–2.

Abdul-Jabbar went on to play six seasons for the Milwaukee Bucks, averaging over thirty points per game. In his second year, 1970–71, Milwaukee won the NBA championship. Abdul-Jabbar averaged 26.6 points and 17 rebounds a game. In 1975, the Los Angeles Lakers made a monstrous deal that changed the landscape of the league. They sent Elmore Smith, Brian Winters, Dave Meyers, and Junior Bridgeman to the Bucks, in exchange for Walt Wesley and Abdul-Jabbar. With the addition of Magic Johnson in 1979–80, the Lakers became the best team in basketball. They won five championships in the 1980s and Abdul-Jabbar was at the center of it all.

On April 5, 1984, Abdul-Jabbar dribbled to the baseline against the Utah Jazz and loosed his Skyhook. With this shot, Abdul-Jabbar passed Wilt Chamberlain as the highest-scoring player in NBA history. Five seasons later, at forty-two, Abdul-Jabbar retired, leaving standards that may never be equaled.

# THE PROFESSIONAL COACH

Coaching in the NBA has its pros and cons. The meal money is terrific, and so is the view from the free seat on the bench. The down side? Let's just say that job security doesn't enter into the equation. When Pat Riley parted ways with the Los Angeles Lakers after the 1989–90 season to pursue a career as a television analyst, he left Detroit Pistons coach Chuck Daly as the senior NBA coach. Daly, who presided over the Pistons

as they attempted to win their third consecutive league championship in 1990–91, was only in his eighth season. The turnover at the top is astonishing. At the beginning of the 1990–91 season, eight of the league's twenty-seven coaches were in their first year with their current club. Seven were in their second year, six in their third, and three in their fourth.

"That's kind of a frightening thing in a lot of ways," said Milwaukee Bucks coach Del Harris. "To a large degree, what we need to do is be a little more patient with coaching. From the ownership level down to the fan level, they have to expect more responsibility from the players for winning. Usually, the players are let off the hook. In the long run, I think the teams that have done best were teams that stuck with coaches. But I don't think I'm going to convince the owners of anything."

Not when average players are making more than a million dollars a year. In baseball, the maxim goes: It's easier to fire the manager than twenty-five players. That's also true in the NBA, although the number of players per team is less than half that. Even when things are going well, coaching an NBA team is no easy job. And it's not only the strategy, the sneaky illegal zone defenses, and the heartbreak of an overtime loss that is so wearing; it's the care and feeding of twelve egos, often each the size of a small Caribbean island. When there is dissension among the bench-sitters and a team goes bad, the coach is generally seen as the messenger of ill-tidings.

# Red Auerbach

There are a few coaches, however, who have been able to buck the trend. Riley and Daly represent the best of the modern breed. They owe a great debt to Arnold Jacob "Red" Auerbach, the man who is universally acclaimed as the best coach in NBA history. In a twenty-season career, Auerbach's teams won a total of 1,037 games and lost only 548, a winning percentage of 65.4. With Auerbach on the sidelines, the Celtics won nine NBA titles. But in a very real sense, Auerbach had a hand in all of the sixteen championship banners that hang from the rafters at Boston Garden.

Born in Brooklyn, New York, on September 20, 1917, Auerbach's early track record did not suggest his future success in basketball. Auerbach was a five-foot-ten (178-cm) guard at Seth Low Junior College and, later, at George Washington University. He did not exactly singe the net, averaging all of six points per game over three seasons. But like the many major-league baseball managers who developed a love and understanding of the game precisely because they were not capable of mastering it, Auerbach channeled his energy into coaching. In the NBA's maiden season, 1946–47, Auerbach coached the Washington Capitols to a 49–11 record, the league's best. After three seasons there and another at Tri-Cities, Auerbach landed in Boston.

Celtics owner Walter Brown desperately needed a savior. Boston had lost far more games than it had won in the franchise's first four years, and he chose Auerbach to turn things around. Auerbach created and nurtured a winning atmosphere that few professional sports franchises have approached. Auerbach's attention to detail, something Riley and Daly would also become noted for, was legendary. In the early

**Sure, Arnold "Red" Auerbach blew a lot of smoke, but he usually backed up what he said. Under Auerbach, the Boston Celtics won eight straight NBA titles, a record that may never be matched.**

1940s, through conversations with New York Yankees short-stop Phil Rizzuto, Auerbach learned of Joe McCarthy's management approach and style and vowed to operate the same way if he ever got the chance.

"[McCarthy] believed the way you acted off the field had a great deal to do with the way you perform on it," Auerbach says. "I decided that any club I ever coached would be imbued with this philosophy: Dress like a champion, act like a champion, and you'll play like a champion. Celtics Pride was no myth, no fairy tale, but pride was a part of what made us what we were. For a player to feel good about his team and teammates, he must also feel good about his role in the team's success."

Although the team became an instant winner, the first championship banner did not come until 1956–57. Just before that season, Auerbach proved himself as a general manager as well as a coach. Looking ahead, Auerbach dealt two of his best players, Ed Macauley and Cliff Hagan, to the St. Louis Hawks for the draft choice that would turn out to be center Bill Russell. With Russell in the pivot, backed by Bob Cousy and Bill Sharman, the Celtics won their first league title by defeating, as fate would have it, St. Louis in seven games.

Two years later, the Celtics won the first of eight consecutive NBA titles, far and away the league record. After the last one, in 1965–66, Auerbach moved upstairs, designating Russell the Celtics' player-coach. As Boston's president, Auerbach kept the Celtics winning. Certainly, Auerbach was blessed with great players, but it was he who discovered most of them in the draft and managed to bring them to Boston. In addition to Russell, his draft picks included Sam Jones, John Havlicek, Jo Jo White, Dave Cowens, Paul Westphal, and in 1978, Larry Bird of Indiana State. Auerbach drafted Bird a year early as a junior-eligible; once again he beat everyone to the punch. Later, there were hopelessly one-sided trades that brought Dennis Johnson, Kevin McHale, and Robert Parrish to the Celtics. That Boston won titles with four different coaches after Auerbach was a tribute to his ability.

And he's still at it well into his seventies. The Celtics continue to be a factor every season and Auerbach is still responsible. Auerbach's book, *Basketball for the Player, the Fan and Coach*, has been translated into seven languages and is the best-selling basketball book in print.

# Pat Riley

In style, Pat Riley could not be more different from Auerbach. For one thing, at six foot four (193 cm) and 205 pounds (93 kg), Riley looks like a basketball player. For another, Riley doesn't habitually smoke victory cigars. In substance, however, the two men are quite similar. Riley coached the Los Angeles Lakers for nine seasons, bringing the team to the championship series seven times. The Lakers won four titles, making Riley's final record of 481–175 the league's best-ever winning percentage, 73.3.

Granted, Riley had Hall of Fame players like Kareem Abdul-Jabbar and Magic Johnson to call on, but he also deftly worked to maintain their concentration amid the glitter of Los Angeles. He did it by being tough, not always making the "popular choice," and by continuously motivating his talented players. "He wants practices harder than games," Abdul-Jabbar once said, "especially after a loss."

Unlike Auerbach, Riley was a fair college player. The son of Leon Riley, a former major-league catcher and minor-league manager, he was born on March 20, 1945, in Rome, New York, and wound up at the University of Kentucky, where he averaged 18.3 points per game over a four-year career. As a professional player, however, Riley was hardly an All-Star. Yet, despite averaging 7.4 points per game over his career, he played for nine seasons, through 1975–76. For six of those seasons, Riley played in Los Angeles. Five years after his career ended as a player, Riley replaced Paul Westead as the Lakers' head coach. That first season, 1981–82, the Lakers finished the regular season with a 57–25 record. Los Angeles torched Phoenix and San Antonio in four straight games in the Western Conference semifinals and finals and beat the Philadelphia 76ers in a six-game championship series. Not bad for a rookie.

After reaching the finals the next two seasons, the Lakers put together one of the great streaks in basketball history over the next four years. They averaged sixty-three victories and won three titles. In January 1990, Riley won his 500th game against Indiana, making him the fastest coach in league history to achieve that milestone. In his last season, for the first time in his coaching career, Riley was named the NBA's Coach of the Year. In 1991–92, Riley ended his brief retirement and signed to coach the New York Knicks.

Pat Riley, a slick presence on the sidelines in Los Angeles, won 500 games faster than any coach in NBA history. Now he's 3,000 miles away, coaching the New York Knicks.

**Chuck Daly's knowledge of the game, his attention to detail, and motivational skills made him the obvious choice to coach the 1992 United States Olympic basketball team.**

# Chuck Daly

Like Riley, Chuck Daly carries himself with confidence, dresses to kill, and knows how to get the most from his players. He guided the Detroit Pistons to back-to-back championships in 1988–89 and 1989–90 and is acknowledged as one of today's masters of strategy and psychology, not necessarily in that order. But it didn't come easily. Charles Joseph Daly succeeded the old-fashioned way: He worked for it.

He was born on July 20, 1930, in St. Mary's, Pennsylvania. Playing briefly at St. Bonaventure before transferring to Bloomsburg State College in 1949, at six foot two (188 cm), 180 pounds (82 kg), Daly was a gritty player if nothing else. His last two seasons yielded a 13.1 point scoring average and a compelling argument that he was not NBA material, at least not as a player. After two years in the army, Daly signed on with Punxsutawney (Pennsylvania) High School. Eight years

later, he convinced Duke University coach Vic Bubas to make him an assistant there. Six years later, Daly succeeded Bob Cousy as the head coach at Boston College. The Eagles were 26–24 in his two seasons there. Daly moved on to the University of Pennsylvania in 1971 and won more than 75 percent of his games. The Philadelphia 76ers head coach Billy Cunningham liked what he saw and brought Daly on as an assistant in 1978, and Daly stayed for four seasons.

When the first offer to head coach in the big leagues came, Daly felt compelled to accept, even though it came from the Cleveland Cavaliers. Forty-one games later, thirty-two of them defeats, Daly was back in Philadelphia, this time as a broadcast analyst. In 1983, the Pistons, who had strung together six consecutive losing seasons, asked Daly to be their head coach. He was fifty-three years old. Naturally, Daly accepted. Suddenly, winning became the norm in Detroit. Daly may have been the only person who wasn't completely surprised.

"I know how hard I've worked in this profession," Daly says. "I know how many times I drove hundreds of miles to hear lectures. I'm one of the few guys old enough to have heard Clair Bee and Frank McGuire and Adolph Rupp. All of them. I know the game. And the people who know me know I know the game."

## THE NBA CHAMPIONSHIP SERIES

For the first six seasons of his glorious career, Michael Jordan achieved every individual goal you could imagine. But one enormous team goal eluded his grasp: the NBA Championship. And then, a remarkable thing happened—Jordan and the Chicago Bulls won the NBA title in 1990–91. And they repeated in 1991–92. And, against great odds, they threepeated in 1992–93. They defeated the Phoenix Suns in six games with an uplifting 99–98 victory to make history. Chicago became only the third NBA team (following the Minneapolis Lakers, 1952–54, and the Boston Celtics, 1959–66) to win three championships in a row.

On June 14, 1990, the Detroit Pistons won their second consecutive NBA title, dispatching the Portland Trail Blazers four games to one. Notably, it was the Pistons' second consecutive league title. This feat had previously been accomplished five other times. Another remarkable thing about the 1989–90 championship series: It did not include the Boston Celtics or Los Angeles Lakers. In forty-four years of the NBA's final best-of-seven series, the Celtics have made a staggering nineteen appearances. Ranking close behind are the Los Angeles Lakers with seventeen. If you factor in the six trips the Minneapolis Lakers made to the finals before the franchise moved west to Los Angeles, the Lakers and Celtics represent forty-two appearances in the league's showcase event, nearly one for every season. The two teams have met head-to-head on ten occasions, with the Celtics winning eight.

The Minneapolis Lakers, led by center George Mikan, was the first team in history to repeat as champion. The 1948–49 Lakers edged Washington four games to two in the final and dispatched Syracuse by the same score the next season. Coach John Kundla's 1950–51 team lost three out of four games to eventual champion Rochester in the Western Divi-

sion finals, but came back with three straight titles. Mikan retired after the third championship, in 1953–54, but Minneapolis wound up in the finals five years later opposite Boston and its young coach, Red Auerbach.

While Kundla and Mikan were putting together a historic three-year run at the top, Auerbach was busy trying to teach the Celtics how to win. In 1956–57, in the league's eleventh year, Boston reached the finals for the first time. The Celtics, led by rookie center Bill Russell, went 44–28 and swept to the finals, opposite St. Louis. The Hawks won the opener in Boston 125–123 in a torrid overtime game and the series never cooled off. The Celtics won the seventh game by the same score, this time with two overtimes. It was the first of sixteen titles for the Celtics. After losing to St. Louis the following year, Boston beat Kundla's Lakers in another stirring seven-game series and went on to win the next year as well. The championship rivalry between Boston and Minneapolis was over, however, because the Lakers moved to Los Angeles in 1961.

One year later, the Celtics and Lakers met in a classic confrontation. It was the 1961–62 final and the Lakers were trying desperately to prevent the Celtics from winning their fourth straight title and breaking their NBA record. Boston had a terrific nucleus of players: Bill Russell, Bob Cousy, Sam Jones, K.C. Jones, Bill Sharmin, Tom Heinsohn, and Frank Ramsey. The Lakers countered with Elgin Baylor and Jerry West. The two teams split the first six games, saving the showpiece for last. The Celtics prevailed 110–107 in overtime at the Boston Garden for their fourth consecutive crown. Amazingly, the Celtics won four more championships, beating Los Angeles in the final three times.

The third of these series, with Boston's eighth straight title at issue, was the pièce de résistance. As you might expect, it came down to a seventh and deciding game. Both teams had changed since their first NBA final meeting four years earlier. Cousy had retired and the Celtics were getting older, so they had picked up some younger legs to run the floor, namely John Havlicek and Don Nelson. The Lakers had added a pair of young players, Gail Goodrich and Walt Hazzard, to help with scoring, but West and Baylor were still the heart of the team. Boston finished the regular season with a record of 54–26, but placed second to the Philadelphia 76ers by one

Next page: Larry Joe Bird can't jump or run particularly fast, but he is one of the most complete players in the history of the game.

game in the Eastern Division. The Celtics struggled to beat the Cincinnati Royals three games to two in the Eastern semifinals, then eliminated the 76ers by winning four games of five. Los Angeles labored to beat St. Louis in a seven-game series. In the finals, the Lakers stole the first two games from the Celtics at Boston Garden including the opener (133–129 in overtime). Boston returned the favor in Los Angeles, and on April 28, 1966, the series was even at three games apiece. The Celtics were battered; all five starters wore some kind of protective wrapping. Russell was slowed by a broken bone in his foot, but played remarkably well in the first half. Baylor and West couldn't take advantage of the ailing center, missing fifteen of eighteen shots from the floor. The Lakers never recovered. The Celtics ran out to a huge lead, then hung on for a 95–93 victory. Both Russell and Havlicek played all forty-eight minutes giving Auerbach a sublime sendoff in his last season as general manager.

The Philadelphia 76ers and Wilt Chamberlain had little trouble eliminating the Celtics in the Eastern Division finals of the 1966–67 season, and officially ended the Boston bid for nine straight championship banners. The 76ers became league champions by beating San Francisco four games to two. With Russell playing and coaching, the Celtics returned in 1967–68 and 1968–69 for two more titles. Predictably, they beat Los Angeles in the finals both times. But after that clinching seventh-game victory on May 5, 1969, the NBA championship was no longer the province of a single team. For the next nineteen seasons, no team was able to defend its league title.

The New York Knicks made a run, reaching three championship series in four years, but in between titles in 1970 and 1973, the Milwaukee Bucks and Lakers claimed victory. After that, parity superceded for a while. Boston won in 1974, followed by Golden State, Boston, Portland, Washington, Seattle, Los Angeles, Boston, Los Angeles, Philadelphia, Boston, Los

Angeles, and Boston. Throughout the tournament's forty-four-year history, the team with the best regular-season record has won twenty-three times, but for eight straight years, the regular-season champion failed to win. The Lakers were clearly the dominant team of the 1980s, however something, namely Boston and the Houston Rockets, got in the way of back-to-back titles. In 1986–87, the Lakers beat the Celtics in the final and prevailed the following season in a seven-game thriller with Detroit to become the first team to repeat since the Celtics of 1968–69.

And what happened next? The Pistons dethroned the Lakers in the 1989 final and managed to repeat the following season by crushing Portland in the championship series. Previously, only the Celtics and Lakers had managed to do it. "We never talked about it all season long," said Detroit guard Isiah Thomas, the MVP of the final series. "We wanted to repeat as champions, but not to prove it to anybody else. We wanted to do it for ourselves."

# THE NBA ALL-STAR GAME

As basketball's popularity has mushroomed in recent years, its annual showcase has gained in stature as well. The NBA All-Star Game at mid-season has become an institution and much, much more than a game, for it now encompasses an entire weekend. It begins on Saturday night and builds to the climactic game on Sunday afternoon. Following is the typical All-Star Game agenda, as was followed at the Charlotte Coliseum on February 9 and 10, 1991.

It began with the legends game, a surprisingly spirited contest between former NBA players. Oscar Robertson, at fifty-two, looked terrific, swishing his first shot of the game. He went on to play seventeen minutes, the highest total among the game's twenty stars selected to represent the East and West Conferences. George Gervin still fired away, making four of eleven shots for the West. Rick Barry was looking good and went three-for-eight from the floor. David Thompson, playing before a friendly North Carolina crowd, scored a game-high twelve points and proved there was still magic in his legs. Thompson led the East to a 41–34 victory, setting the stage for the three-point contest.

Larry Bird of the Boston Celtics, a crisp three-point shooter, emphatically won the long-distance shooting exhibition when it was first introduced in 1986 helping it to gain national attention. In 1991, defending champion Craig Hodges obliterated the field, joining Bird as the only two-time champion. This little-used Chicago Bulls guard shot past Portland guard Terry Porter in the final, 17–12, but his semifinal performance forced the Charlotte crowd to its feet. Hodges connected on his first nineteen three-point shots, breaking Bird's previous record of eleven straight, set in the final round of the 1986 competition.

The evening's finale was the slam-dunk event. The smallest player in the competition, six-foot-one (185-cm) Dee Brown, came away the surprise winner. The Boston Celtics rookie showed incredible leaping ability, combined with a creative flair that pushed him past Seattle's Shawn Kemp, the six-foot-ten (208-cm) pre-contest favorite, in the final. He threw down a spread-eagled reverse jam that scored high with the distinguished judges (who included Julius Erving, Bobby Jones, Dan Roundfield, and George Gervin). And saving the best for last, Brown ran straight at the basket, elevated, closed his eyes, put his free arm over his eyes, and slammed the ball down perfectly. "It was," said Kemp, "the most incredible dunk I ever saw." For his efforts, Brown took home $20,000, a gold trophy, and the respect of his peers.

The game? Ah yes, the game. All-Star Games are basically for showing off, and basketball provides a terrific theater. The league takes it all very seriously, as Charles Barkley will tell you. A foot injury forced the Philadelphia 76ers forward to miss a host of regular-season games, but he came back earlier than expected to rally his flagging teammates. Barkley, a perennial All-Star, figured he'd play four regular-season games before the three-day All-Star break during which he'd rest his aching foot. League officials managed to change his mind. A terse phone call from an NBA executive suggested he make himself available for the game. Barkley carped a bit, but he played in the game. Scoring seventeen points and pulling down twenty-two rebounds, Barkley dominated the annual classic, as the Eastern Conference edged the Western Conference 116–114 in the game's forty-first anniversary. Sure, there were a mind-boggling fifty-one turnovers, but the game came down to the last shot. Fortunately for the East, Kevin Johnson's would-be three-pointer was intercepted by teammate Karl Malone, for reasons he still doesn't understand. "I don't know," said the Utah forward, "but it looked pretty good. I don't actually know why I did what I did. I wasn't trying to pay off the bookies in Vegas or anything."

Scan the list of All-Star records and it reads like a Who's Who of basketball. Kareem Abdul-Jabbar leads all players with eighteen appearances. Next? Wilt Chamberlain, Bob Cousy, and John Havlicek, with thirteen each. Abdul-Jabbar (251 points) is the all-time leading scorer, followed by Oscar Robertson (246), Bob Pettit (224), and Julius Erving (221). The two best scoring averages belong to, surprisingly, Phoenix Suns forward Tom Chambers (23.0) and Michael Jordan of the Chicago Bulls (20.6). Magic Johnson is first in assists (115), Isiah Thomas leads in steals (26), and Abdul-Jabbar is the leading shot-blocker (31). Stars, all.

# THE CONTINENTAL BASKETBALL ASSOCIATION

Consider the travails and travels of Kevin Douglas Gamble, basketball player. After playing at both Lincoln College (Illinois) and the University of Iowa, Gamble was the third-round choice of the Portland Trail Blazers in the 1987 draft. The six-foot-five (196-cm) guard/forward made the team but lasted only nine games into the season. Gamble was waived on December 9, 1987, and turned to the safety net for fallen NBA players and rising stars, the Continental Basketball Association. He played in forty games for the Quad City Thunder, averaging 21 points, 5.9 rebounds, and 3.7 assists. Gamble, who was third in the CBA's Rookie of the Year voting, then spent the off season playing for the Añejo Rum team in the Philippines. He began the next season with Quad City and was the league's leading scorer, with an average of 27.8 points, when the Boston Celtics signed him after twelve CBA games. His numbers (187 points in forty-four games) were not impressive, but Gamble had made it into the NBA for good. Playing with Larry Bird, Robert Parrish, and Kevin McHale clearly elevated his game.

Two seasons later, at the All-Star break in 1991, Gamble led the NBA in shooting percentage. In fact, his average from the floor hovered around 60 percent all season long. "I always thought I could play in this league, I never thought I couldn't," says Gamble. "It was just a question of getting playing time to prove it. Now, I'm at the point where I want to make them say, 'Hey, we can't take Kevin out.' That's the way it has to be to get minutes on this kind of team."

Gamble is just another example of a CBA alumnus making good. The list includes Tony Campbell and Tod Murphy of the Minnesota Timberwolves, Michael Adams of the Denver Nuggets, and Golden State's Rod Higgins. Since the college game is so well organized, basketball does not require baseball's elaborate minor-league system. The CBA, basketball's only minor league, is all the NBA needs. "Our league is a league of opportunity," says CBA Commissioner Irv Kaze. "If they want to get to the NBA, this is the quickest way to do it. The NBA sees them and knows them. The NBA scouts our games and gets our tapes. The NBA keeps a pulse on our league."

The numbers back him up. During the 1989–90 season, no fewer than twenty-nine CBA players were called up by NBA teams, and in March 1990, there were a record fifty-nine former CBA players on NBA rosters. The relationship works well for both sides. The NBA signed a $2.7 million player and referee development deal in 1990 with the CBA. And the level of basketball is impressive enough to support fourteen teams in places like Albany, New York; Cedar Rapids, Iowa; La Crosse, Wisconsin; and Pensacola, Florida. For the eighth straight season, the CBA set a league attendance record (1,438,604) in 1989–90, with ten franchises averaging attendance of more than 2,700 per game. On February 4, 1990, 11,272 fans jammed the new Knickerbocker Arena in Albany for a Patroons game, a league record. The blend of young talent and experienced hands can make for compelling action.

In Santa Barbara, fans had been treated to the scoring theatrics of Derrick Gervin, the league's leading scorer (31.7 points), until the New Jersey Nets called him up. Gervin, twenty-six, averaged twelve points per game in his twenty-one games in the NBA in the 1990 season. At the same time his brother George, who had won four NBA scoring titles while playing for San Antonio, was laboring for the CBA team in Quad Cities. George Gervin averaged 20.3 points in fourteen CBA games before heading to Europe to play at the age of thirty-eight.

© Jim Gund/Allsport

Is that a sly smile on Clyde Drexler's face as he guards Dominique Wilkins? Probably. Unlike baseball's serious-minded annual all-star game, the NBA contest resembles a dazzling pickup game.

There is something about college basketball's Final Four that stops the nation's sporting clock. Fans, even players, jump up and down as March Madness takes hold.

# THE COLLEGE GAME

The beauty of college basketball is that the best teams often win. In 1985, a scrappy Villanova squad stunned Georgetown, a heavy favorite, 66-64 in the NCAA final.

© R. Mackson/FPG International

**As a collegian at Cincinnati, Oscar Robertson led the nation in scoring three consecutive seasons but the national title eluded the Bearcats.**

© Manny Rubio

# THE GREAT COLLEGE PLAYERS

College basketball is exciting and wonderfully unpredictable. Players are generally shorter than in the NBA, so the smaller players are able to have a greater impact. Zone defenses are legal, which encourages more passing and perimeter shooting. There are some 270 schools fielding NCAA Division I basketball teams these days, and on a given afternoon, an unknown, unranked team can beat a heavily favored team ranked high in the national polls. Great players seem to come from nowhere. For every Oscar Robertson and Pete Maravich, there is a scoring champion like Kevin Houston of Army (32.0 points per game in 1987) or Zam Fredrick of South Carolina (28.9 points per game in 1981).

Making a mark at the collegiate level is no guarantee of a successful professional career. Still, it doesn't hurt. Of the seven extraordinary college players profiled below, four—Robertson, Maravich, Elvin Hayes, and Bill Bradley—went on to great professional careers and are already in the Basketball Hall of Fame. Bill Walton, who helped UCLA continue its dynasty through the early 1970s, was named the NBA's Most Valuable Player in 1978 and owns two championship rings. Injuries, however, prevented Walton from reaching his glorious potential. As a professional, Austin Carr of Notre Dame scored more points in an NCAA Tournament game (sixty-one versus Ohio in 1970) than any other player and remains second only to Maravich in career scoring average (34.6 points per game), but his professional career was less memorable. Less than ethereal, Carr averaged a respectable 15.4 points per game over ten seasons. Danny Manning of Kansas, the second-leading scorer in NCAA Tournament history, sandwiched between Hayes and Robertson, was the MVP of the 1988 tourney. He is only beginning to blossom as a player for the Los Angeles Clippers.

The following are the magnificent seven, listed in chronological order.

# Oscar Robertson

Oscar Palmer Robertson was the first player to lead the nation's NCAA Division I scorers three seasons in a row. Frank Selvy and Darrell Floyd, both of Furman University, locked up the scoring title two years each, back-to-back (1953–56), but Robertson went them one better. He was a six-foot-five (196-cm), 220-pound (100-kg) guard who was equally comfortable shooting, rebounding, and passing. He just happened to be better at shooting. Or was it passing? Or rebounding? Robertson may have been the most versatile college player to ever play the game.

Born on November 24, 1938, in Charlotte, Tennessee, Robertson moved to Indianapolis when he was young. Immediately consumed by Indiana's prevailing passion, Robertson was recognized as a future college star as early as his junior year at Crispus Attucks High School. As a senior in 1956, he led his team to two state titles and was named Indiana Player of the Year. Robertson proceeded to the University of Cincinnati, and after a season with the freshman team, he began to rewrite the NCAA record book. Robertson had everything: speed, power, peripheral vision, soft hands, and an uncanny ability to catalyze his four teammates. As a sophomore in 1957–58, Robertson averaged 35.1 points per game and 15.2 rebounds per game. He shot 57 percent from the floor, an astounding figure for a guard. In the NCAA Tournament, Robertson burned Arkansas for fifty-six points in a regional third-place game, the third-highest tournament performance on record.

Surrounded by a better cast of players the next two seasons, Robertson's scoring numbers fell off slightly. His scoring

© Manny Rubio

and rebounding averages were 32.6 points and 16.3 in 1958–59, but the Bearcats went farther in post-season play. Cincinnati won two games to advance to the Final Four before losing to the eventual champion, the University of California, and finishing third overall. As a senior, Robertson averaged 33.7 points and 14.1 rebounds, and Cincinnati finished third in the nation for the second consecutive year. With Robertson averaging 33.8 points per game over three seasons, the Bearcats won eighty-nine games and lost only nine. Maravich and Carr are the only college players with better career scoring averages, and they didn't begin to rebound or pass on Robertson's level; when he was finished, Robertson held fourteen NCAA records.

As fate would have it, when Robertson turned professional, Cincinnati broke through and won the national title two years in a row. Playing for the Cincinnati Royals and Milwaukee Bucks, Robertson captured many individual honors, such as Rookie of the Year (1961), League MVP (1964), All-Star MVP (1961, 1964, 1969), and the all-time assists record of 9,887. He achieved only a single NBA title with the Milwaukee Bucks in 1971.

## Bill Bradley

Three years after Robertson left Cincinnati, college basketball had a new, similarly versatile star. His name was Bill Bradley, and he could shoot, rebound, and pass. Like Robertson, he was six foot five (196 cm) and maneuvered with skill among the taller players under the basket.

Bradley was born on July 28, 1943, in Crystal City, Missouri, and began playing basketball at the age of nine. His wearying daily practices paid off when he scored 3,066 points as a two-year High School All-America at Crystal City High School. Bradley was intelligent on the court and off and enrolled at Princeton University in 1962. In his first varsity season, Bradley helped lead the Tigers to an NCAA Tournament berth and began to build a magnificent post-season. Three years later, Bradley had scored 303 tournament points, the second-highest total at the time, placing him behind only Robertson. Bradley's scoring average in nine games was a point better

**Bill Bradley became the first college basketball player to win the Sullivan Award as the nation's outstanding amateur athlete.**

Almost single-handedly, Houston's Elvin Hayes won "The Game of the Century," outplaying UCLA's Lew Alcindor.

than Robertson's and was surpassed only by Austin Carr of Notre Dame.

The next season, Princeton advanced to the second round of the tournament. Later that year, Bradley was a member of the 1964 gold-medal-winning U.S. Olympic basketball team. Bradley's senior season was epic. His complementary skills as a team player were evident as Princeton moved through the tournament field. The Tigers reached the semifinals, but fell to Michigan, 93–76. In the consolation game for third place, Bradley shook loose. He scored fifty-eight points in an easy victory over Wichita State, which surpassed Robertson's previous tournament record of fifty-six. Today, only Carr's sixty-one-point explosion against Ohio ranks higher.

Bradley finished his three-year college career with a number of records. His scoring average of 30.2 points is sixteenth on the all-time list. He became the third player in NCAA history to produce more than 2,000 points (2,503) and 1,000 (1,008) rebounds in a career. Bradley also became the first basketball player to win the Sullivan Award, for the nation's outstanding amateur athlete. He then turned down a lucrative professional offer in 1965 to pursue his education at Oxford University. Two years later, Bradley signed with the New York Knicks, scored 9,217 points in ten seasons, and was part of two championship teams. Basketball was only a stepping stone for Bradley, however. Today, he is a highly respected U.S. Senator from New Jersey.

# Elvin Hayes

To begin with, Elvin Ernest Hayes was one of the best professional basketball players ever. He ranks third on the all-time NBA scoring list with 27,313 points and fourth in rebounding, with 16,279. Although only one player in league history, Kareem Abdul-Jabbar, played more than Hayes' sixteen seasons, his most important contribution to basketball came in his college years at the University of Houston.

The same season Bill Bradley left the college game, Hayes came blazing in. He was born on November 17, 1945, in Rayville, Louisiana, and played there at Eula D. Britton High School. Hayes, who would grow to six foot nine (206 cm) and 235 pounds (107 kg), was a fierce competitor with the rare combination of speed and power that allowed him to score and rebound, seemingly at will. At Houston, Hayes averaged some ridiculous numbers for the freshman team, 25.1 points and 23.8 rebounds. His scoring increased gradually each year, and the Cougars, with help from Hayes' teammate Don Chaney, improved, too. In 1967, Houston finished third in the NCAA Tournament, losing to UCLA in the semifinals, and great things were predicted for 1967–68, when Hayes and Chaney would be seniors. Meanwhile, at UCLA, John Wooden's team was in the process of winning seven consecutive titles.

It was Houston coach Guy Lewis who first recognized the marketing possibilities of the game between the two teams scheduled for January 20, 1968. He convinced school and local officials to move the game from Houston's tiny on-campus facility to the grand Houston Astrodome. Billed as the Game of the Century, ticket requests mounted as the event neared. UCLA came in with a forty-seven-game winning streak, but it seemed Houston had a viable chance to win. The media coverage was incredible. Even more amazing, the game was as good as the hype had promised.

With 52,693 spectators in the seats, Hayes' matchup with celebrated UCLA center Lew Alcindor was a mismatch. Hayes scored twenty-nine points in the first half, sinking fourteen of nineteen shots from the field. He also blocked several of Alcindor's shots. With forty-four seconds left, the game was tied at sixty-nine. It was Hayes who won it, 71–69, with a pair of free throws. He finished with thirty-nine points, fifteen rebounds, and eight blocked shots. Alcindor, who had scratched his cor-

nea a week earlier, scored only fifteen points. In three seasons, Hayes played in thirteen NCAA Tournament games, finishing as the career leader in points scored (358) and rebounding average (17.1).

Although Hayes would go on to a professional career that most players could only dream about, his performance in the Game of the Century ignited a national following for college basketball.

# Pete Maravich

Like Robertson and Bradley before him, Maravich stood six foot five (196 cm) and was dazzlingly dexterous. Robertson saw the floor better and rebounded with more force and Bradley probably improved his teammates more, but Maravich was breathtaking to behold. He could snap a behind-the-back pass and dribble through traffic with ease.

"I don't like to wait for momentum to generate itself," he once said. "Ever since high school, I've found that I can sometimes get my team hot with a behind-the-back pass or a razzle-dazzle drive, one of the plays that people sometimes call me a hotdog for trying. I'm making those plays with a purpose, not showboating. I make those plays I know I can make because I've practiced them and practiced them."

More than anything and anyone, Maravich could score. That's why they called him Pistol Pete. The son of a basketball coach, he was born on June 22, 1947, in Aliquippa, Pennsylvania. In high school, Maravich worked tirelessly in the gym, perfecting his shot and the moves that would bring him fame. After playing at three different schools in North and South Carolina, Maravich joined his father, Press, at Louisiana State University. In three varsity seasons, Pistol Pete would toss up scoring numbers that have yet to be equaled.

In 1967–68, Maravich averaged a phenomenal 43.8 points per game, led the nation in scoring, and was named to the All-America Team. He somehow managed to improve as a junior and senior, averaging 44.2 points per game in 1968–69 and 44.5 in 1969–70 in his assault on the record book. In that final season, Maravich scored fifty points or more ten times and totaled 1,381 points, a college single-season record. When his college career was over, Maravich had set new NCAA stan-

© Naismith Memorial Basketball Hall of Fame

dards for points (3,667), scoring average (44.2), field goals (1,387), and free throws (893). On twenty-eight occasions, he scored fifty points or more, another record. To put Maravich's scoring prowess in perspective, his 44.2 points per game are nearly ten points more than the next-best average.

Maravich went on to play with the Atlanta Hawks, the New Orleans Jazz, and the Boston Celtics. In 658 games, he averaged 24.1 points. He was a five-time All-Star and led the NBA in scoring in 1977 with an average of 31.1. On January 5, 1988, basketball lost one of its brightest lights when Maravich died suddenly at the age of forty.

## Austin Carr

The great players seem to become greater when their team needs them most. Austin Carr, the six-foot-three (190-cm),

200-pound (91-kg) scorer, was always there for Notre Dame. Quite simply, Carr was the greatest clutch scorer in NCAA Tournament history. His scoring average in seven post-season games is a giddy 41.3, and three of the tournament's five highest-scoring games came from his hands.

You could see him coming. Carr scored 2,124 points at Macklin High School in Washington, D.C., and arrived at the South Bend campus in 1968 with a reputation for scoring. After Carr fired in fifty-two points in a freshman game against Michigan State, people couldn't wait for his first tour of duty with the varsity team. A recurring broken foot curtailed his playing time and left Irish fans looking toward Carr's final two seasons and he didn't disappoint anyone.

Consider his consistent excellence: In his last two seasons at Notre Dame, 1969–70 and 1970–71, Carr played in fifty-eight games and scored over forty points twenty-three times, more than thirty points forty-six times, and was never held under twenty. His point totals of 1,106 (38.1 points per game) and 1,101 (38.0) are the sixth and seventh all-time best in NCAA history. As a junior, Carr torched Ohio for sixty-one points in the first round of the NCAA Tournament, a total that remains the standard today. In the second round, Carr scored fifty-two points against Kentucky. In a consolation game, Carr gunned in forty-five against Iowa. Carr could score inside with power, outside with touch, and use either hand with skill.

Carr's most memorable performance came in his final Notre Dame season at home against mighty UCLA. The Bruins had already won four consecutive NCAA titles, but with Carr scoring heavily from drives to the basket and shots from the baseline, Notre Dame took a thirteen point lead. UCLA came back to even the score at forty-seven all early in the second half. Carr simply took over after that. He scored fifteen of Notre Dame's final seventeen points and the Irish prevailed, 89–82. Carr had scored forty-six points in UCLA's only defeat of the season. In the NCAA Tournament that season, Carr scored fifty-two points against Texas Christian in the first round and, later, seared Houston for forty-seven points.

Not surprisingly, Carr was the first overall choice in the 1971 NBA draft. He averaged 21.2 points as a rookie for the Cleveland Cavaliers. In ten professional seasons, Carr averaged 15.4 points per game.

# Bill Walton

The same genetic factors that pushed Bill Walton to the towering height of six foot eleven (211 cm) probably cut short his career. He grew six inches (15 cm) between his freshman and sophomore seasons at Helix High School in La Mesa, California. Walton stretched three more inches (8 cm) the following year and his knees were never the same; they were susceptible to injury for the rest of his playing days. As a fifteen-year-old, he had his first knee operation to repair a torn cartilage.

Before tendonitis ravaged his knees and cut his professional career short, you could see Walton, born November 5, 1952, in all his glory at UCLA. He was a dominant center in high school, producing a forty-nine-game winning streak with Helix, when UCLA coach John Wooden recruited him. (It didn't hurt that Bill's older brother Bruce, a six-foot-five [196-cm], 265-pound [120-kg] tackle, was already playing football at UCLA.) Walton fit the Wooden mold: talented, aggressive, and unselfish. While Walton played freshman basketball in 1970–71, the Bruins were in the process of winning their fifth consecutive NCAA championship. What followed was one of the greatest college careers in history.

Walton averaged 18.1 points and 15.5 rebounds as UCLA won all thirty of its games in 1971–72, including the NCAA Tournament final over Florida State. Not only was he named the Player of the Year, but Walton was also honored as the tournament's Most Outstanding Player. And then it happened again, in precisely the same way. UCLA was 30–0 in 1972–73 and Walton averaged 21.1 points and 16.9 rebounds. Once again, Walton was the Player of the Year and once again, UCLA reached the NCAA Tournament final. The difference this time around was that Walton raised the level of his game to an astounding height. In the memorable championship game against Memphis State, Walton shot at the basket twenty-two times and made twenty-one field goals, for a shooting percentage of 95.5. To put that in perspective, note that James Worthy's 13-for-17 (76.5 percent) for North Carolina against Georgetown in 1982 is the next best finals effort. Walton added two free throws for a total of forty-four points and thirteen rebounds as UCLA won its seventh straight title, 87–66. For the entire tournament, Walton made forty-five of fifty-nine shots (76.3 percent) to set a new tourney record for field-goal percentage. His three-year career percentage of 68.6 is also an NCAA record.

And when Walton's perfect game was over, Memphis State coach Gene Bartow sighed and said, "There goes the greatest college player of all time."

# Danny Manning

The NCAA Tournament's all-time scoring list is a thing of beauty. There is Elvin Hayes at the top, with 358 points, and not far behind are Oscar Robertson (324), Lew Alcindor (304), Bill Bradley (303), Austin Carr (289), Jerry West (275), and Bill Walton (256). To some basketball fans the second name on the list might come as a surprise: Danny Manning, Kansas, 328 points. Cynics will point out that Manning accumulated that gaudy total over four seasons, while players like Hayes, Robertson, and Alcindor played only three seasons because freshmen were ineligible to play varsity games in their day.

Regardless, Manning's name belongs among the best in college history. He was born in Hattiesburg, Mississippi, on May 17, 1966, and played high school basketball in North Carolina and Kansas. As a freshman playing on the varsity team at the University of Kansas, the six-foot-ten (208-cm) center displayed a smooth shooting touch and averaged 14.6 points per game. As a sophomore, Manning averaged 16.7 points per game and shot 60 percent from the floor. In fourteen Big Eight games, his shooting percentage was a torrid 66.7, a league record. His scoring average rose to 23.0 in 1986–87, and Manning scored forty-two points against Southwest Missouri State in the second round of the NCAA Tournament.

In 1987–88, Manning became the leader that Kansas coach Larry Brown had long envisioned. Brown's contention had been that Manning was sometimes too unselfish and was sometimes too willing to pass when he had an open shot. Manning averaged 24.8 points per game and took charge in the 1988 NCAA Tournament. In the final against favored Oklahoma, Manning scored thirty-one points, ripped down eighteen rebounds, and added five assists in a wonderfully complete performance. Kansas won 83–79, and Manning was named the tournament's Outstanding Player. In four years, Manning produced 2,951 points and 1,187 rebounds.

© David Klutho/Allsport USA

The Los Angeles Clippers made Manning the first player selected in the 1988 NBA draft. Through twenty-nine games of the 1988–89 season, he was averaging 16.7 points per game, but going up for a layup at Milwaukee's Bradley Center he tore the anterior cruciate ligament in his right knee. Manning came back faster than expected, and in seventy-one games the following season, Manning averaged 16.3 points and seemed to have picked up where he left off at Kansas.

## THE GREAT COLLEGE COACHES

Coaching a college basketball team can be a daunting enterprise. A college team's success is based on strong recruiting, which requires sound judgment and hard work, as well as personality and character. Holding the attention of eighteen-year-olds is no easy matter; teaching them to maintain their poise in front of 15,000 fans is even more difficult. The man who can do all this and, furthermore, coach a group of ten to the sport's highest level year after year is a rarity. The following eight coaches proved themselves masters at their profession. Four of them are still at it. Experience, it seems, is the best teacher.

Adolph Rupp was at the University of Kentucky for forty-one years, where he won 875 games, the all-time record. F.C. "Phog" Allen coached for forty-six seasons, most of them at the University of Kansas. Ray Meyer coached at DePaul University for forty-two seasons and won 724 games. John Wooden, who spent twenty-seven years at UCLA, fashioned ten NCAA teams in a span of twelve years. The new breed of coaches is similarly single-minded. Dean Smith has been a fixture at North Carolina since 1962, and Bobby Knight has worn the red sweater of Indiana University since 1972, the same season Wooden assistant Denny Crum took over at Louisville where he still coaches today. John Thompson arrived at Georgetown in 1973.

About coaching college basketball, Knight says: "There have been three coaches, in terms of the game's technical aspects, who heavily influenced coaching college basketball. Number one, Claire Bee, two, Henry Iba, and three, Pete Newell. It all started with Bee and then Iba came up with some defensive help theories. Pete had more to do with bringing a pressure style of defensive play than any coach in history. Those two guys formed the basic style of defense that you see today. They were running second screen cuts before anybody. Most kids today haven't ever heard of a second screen cut."

In any case, coaching a college team is infinitely more difficult than watching the game from the bench. A successful coach like Clarence "Big House" Gaines who has coached at Winston-Salem State College, an NCAA Division II program in North Carolina, for forty-three years, with a staggering 791–384 record, may make it seem easy. But like Allen, Wooden, Smith, and the others, Gaines would agree that coaching a college basketball team is hard; the good coaches just make it look easy.

## F.C. "Phog" Allen

The eager basketball player sought out his coach and told him he, too, wanted to coach college basketball. The coach frowned. "You don't coach basketball, Forrest; you play it."

The player was Forrest Clare Allen, a three-time letterman for the Kansas Jayhawks from 1905–07. The coach was the legendary James Naismith, who invented basketball. Fortunately, Allen didn't take his mentor seriously. When Naismith stepped aside in 1907 after compiling a 55–60 record, Allen was named his successor. Allen left Kansas to coach at Baker University, Haskell Institute, and Central Missouri State University. In seven years at Central Missouri, Allen's combined record was 102–7. In 1919, he returned to his alma mater as athletic director and basketball and football coach. By the time Allen retired in 1956, Kansas had become a national power. In thirty-nine seasons with the Jayhawks, Allen won 590 games and lost 219. Kansas won twenty-four conference championships and appeared in the NCAA championship game three times, winning in 1953. Allen coached fourteen All-Americas. He suffered only two losing seasons.

As dazzling as the statistics are, Allen's greatest contributions came off the court. He was the co-founder of the National Association of Basketball Coaches in 1927 and served as its first president. He was named the National Coach of the Year in 1950 and was enshrined at the Basketball Hall of Fame in 1959. For nearly a decade, he tried to convince Olympic officials that basketball belonged in the international athletic festival. The sport was finally accepted in 1936. Sixteen years later, Allen was an assistant coach of a U.S. Olympic team largely composed of Kansas players. Allen was also instrumental in creating the NCAA Tournament, which began in 1939. And today, Kansas plays its games in the Allen Field House.

In forty-six seasons, Allen's teams won a total of 771 games, a record that stood for years until one of his pupils came along and broke it. His name was Adolph Rupp.

## Adolph Rupp

Just as Allen learned the intricacies of the game from Naismith, the game's creator, so Rupp could accredit Allen. Rupp, a native of Halstead, Kansas, played under Allen at Kansas and was part of the 1922 and 1923 Helms National Championship teams. Rupp had spent hours discussing basketball theory with Allen and got his coaching start in Burr Oak, Kansas, where the only available place to play was the ice skating rink. His experience at Marshalltown High School (Iowa) was similar; not knowing anything about wrestling, he purchased a book and guided his team to the state title. Rupp then moved to Freeport, Illinois, where he produced a 67–16 record. In 1931, he was hired to coach the University of Kentucky for an annual salary of $2,800.

Rupp fashioned an up-tempo, fast-breaking offense, with gritty man-to-man defense. Kentucky won its first ten games under Rupp, finished 15–3, and became the talk of the South. Rupp first reached the Final Four in 1942, when the team finished in a tie for third. His team's next four visits were more fruitful, however. Kentucky won the NCAA championship in 1948, 1949, 1951, and 1958. Rupp ultimately reached the Final Four six times, a figure exceeded only by John Wooden and Dean Smith. Rupp's coaching career, forty-one seasons at Kentucky, was itself an unprecedented record. He was forced to retire in 1972.

**Opposite: Danny Manning's numbers made him one of the most dominant players in college history, but a serious knee injury limited his impact on the professional game.**

© Naismith Memorial Basketball Hall of Fame

problem. And don't we always respect those teachers who demand the most from us? A friend is not just someone who says nice things to us all the time. It's someone who sees the best in us and wants to help us be what we want to be and what we can be."

## Ray Meyer

Born in Chicago on December 18, 1913, Ray Meyer was an All-City player for two years at St. Patrick's High School and moved on to Notre Dame, where he captained the team for two years. He worked as George Keogan's assistant at Notre Dame for two seasons before Keogan recommended him for the vacant head coaching position at DePaul University in 1942. It was the only head coaching job he would ever have.

In forty-two seasons at DePaul, Meyer produced a record of 724–354, for a winning percentage of 67.1. The victories put him fifth on the all-time list, behind Rupp, Allen, Henry Iba (Oklahoma State), and Ed Diddle (Western Kentucky). Meyer's teams posted winning records in thirty-seven seasons and earned invitations to post-season tournaments twenty times, including thirteen NCAA Tournament berths.

Meyer's greatest success came in his later years. The charisma that led many basketball fans to refer to him simply as "Coach," contributed to his excellent recruiting record. And like the best coaches, Meyer was a teacher first. His most notable teams in his early coaching years were the 1943 team that tied for third in the NCAA Tournament and the 1945 NIT champions (a title that came at a time when the NIT was considered more prestigious than the NCAA). His later accomplishments include guiding the Blue Devils to the Final Four in Salt Lake City, Utah, in 1979.

In his final seven seasons, DePaul won 180 games and lost only thirty (a winning percentage of 85.7) and made seven consecutive post-season appearances. Meyer received four National Coach of the Year awards during that time. In 1984, at the height of his success, Meyer handed the team over to his son, Joey. Meyer continues in fund-raising efforts for DePaul and serves as a radio commentator for the team whose image he helped shape.

**Adolph Rupp embraced the basketball philosophy of F.C. "Phog" Allen, who in turn learned the game from Dr. James Naismith. Rupp's Kentucky teams won 875 games and lost only 190, a winning percentage of 82.**

His teams won 875 games and lost only 190, for a winning percentage of 82.2. To this day, Allen's total of 771 is the distant second-place entry. Only Clair Bee and Jerry Tarkanian won more often, but those numbers were generated over the relatively brief span of twenty-one seasons. Rupp's teams won the Southeast Conference twenty-seven times and there were twenty-two All-Americas on his rosters. In 1948, he was the coach of the gold-medal-winning U.S. Olympic team. He was named National Coach of the Year four times, and in all of his years as a coach, Rupp never experienced a losing season.

Rupp was tough on his players, but always toughest on himself. He weathered serious health problems over the years and sometimes coached when it wasn't advisable. On December 10, 1977, at the age of seventy-six, Rupp died. Pastor D. Glynn Burke presided over the burial in Lexington, Kentucky. "He built a tradition of basketball known around the world for excellence," Burke said. "He made us prouder to be Kentuckians. We live in a permissive society in which parents are afraid to discipline their children. Coach Rupp never had that

# John Wooden

John Wooden never even had a chance. "You couldn't grow up in Indiana," he says, "and not have basketball touch you in some way."

Born in Martinsville, Indiana, Wooden's first hoop was a tomato basket with the bottom knocked out, nailed to the family barn. Wooden made the All-State team his last three years at Martinsville High School. He was the five-foot-ten (178-cm) captain at Purdue University and a three-time Helms All-America. In 1932, Wooden set a Big Ten scoring record on Purdue's national championship team and was named the nation's College Player of the Year. After college, he starred for the Kautsky Grocers of Indianapolis and once made 138 straight free throws in competition, a statistic that underlines Wooden's attention to detail. And then his career really took off.

Coaching was the next logical step. Wooden was a terrific player.(he was enshrined in the Basketball Hall of Fame for his playing prowess) who also understood the value of unselfishness and patience. He first began to preach team basketball as the coach at Dayton (Kentucky) High School and Central High School in South Bend, Indiana. An eleven-year high school record of 218–42 netted him the head coaching job at Indiana

**John Wooden's UCLA teams won an astounding ten NCAA championships in twelve years.**

© Naismith Memorial Basketball Hall of Fame

State University. Two years later, in 1948, Wooden was hired at UCLA. It took time, but Wooden built a winning team of unprecedented quality.

UCLA reached the Final Four for the first time in 1962, placing fourth. In 1964, the Bruins returned to the NCAA Tournament's elite circle and did it right. Wooden's UCLA team would win ten collegiate championships in the next twelve seasons, including seven in a row, before he retired in 1975. Wooden's teams won 667 games, ranking seventh on the all-time list. Six times, Wooden was honored as the National Coach of the Year, and with good reason. Certainly, he had gifted players like Kareem Abdul-Jabbar, Bill Walton, Sidney Wicks, and Gail Goodrich, but he always managed to make them better.

Wooden's success came from an unbeatable teaching formula: explanation, demonstration, correction, and repetition. That's why he always liked the practices better than the games themselves. Cervantes wrote, "The journey is better than the end," and Wooden believes that firmly.

"I appreciated that notion more later, after we started to win championships," he says. "The saying that it's tougher to stay on top than to get there, I don't believe it. It's very tough to get there. And along the way you learn, as Lincoln would say, not just what to do, but what not to do. People say we could never win those championships again, what with parity. But I'm not so sure it couldn't happen today. Winning breeds winning."

## Dean Smith

Wooden's record of twelve Final Four appearances seems unassailable, but there is Dean Smith all alone in second place, with seven trips to the Final Four. This is no accident; Smith has an enviable pedigree.

He was born in Topeka, Kansas, and played high school basketball there before joining Phog Allen's Kansas Jayhawks in 1950. Like Adolph Rupp, he had one of the best teachers possible. Smith played on Allen's 1952 NCAA championship team and joined Air Force as an assistant coach in 1954 before moving on to North Carolina for another three-year assis-

tant's stint. He was promoted to head coach in 1960, succeeding Frank McGuire, who had coached the Tar Heels to the national championship in 1957.

Smith took the patterned offense Allen had used and elevated it to a game involving quick continuity. When North Carolina found itself ahead late in the game, which was often, Smith employed the spread-out Four Corners offense as a way to effectively kill the clock.

Smith's first trip to the Final Four as a coach came in 1967, when the Tar Heels placed fourth. Thus, Smith became one of only five men to play and coach in the Final Four. That appearance began an incredible run of consistency for North Carolina. The Tar Heels made the Final Four seven times in sixteen seasons. As those appearances mounted, Smith was seen as a coach who couldn't win the big game, but his patient philosophy never wavered. "If you make every game a life-and-death thing, you're going to have problems," he said. "You'll be dead a lot."

Smith and North Carolina finally broke through in 1982, when freshman Michael Jordan helped shoot down Georgetown, 63–62, in a memorable championship final. Smith's Tar Heels were the NCAA's fourth-best team in the 1970s and the leading winners (281–63) in the 1980s, a tribute to Smith's brilliance. Through 1992, he had won 740 games, making him the leading winner among active coaches.

## Bobby Knight

The towering numbers haven't piled up for Bobby Knight. Not yet, anyway. For the record, he had won 588 games and lost 210 for a winning percentage of 73.7 through 1992. Of course, Knight is just a kid compared to some of the old coaching masters. Knight was among the youngest coaches to achieve 200 victories (at thirty-five), 300 victories (at age forty), 400 victories (at age forty-four), and 500 victories (at age forty-eight). Only Henry Iba reached 500 victories at a younger age. By the time Knight finishes his career, his record should be comparable to Iba's.

Like Smith, Knight was a player on a national championship team (Ohio State, 1960). He began his coaching career at

© Allsport

**While volatile Bobby Knight's ways and means have come under fire over the years, his results have never been questioned. Only Henry Iba reached 500 victories at a younger age.**

Army, where the Cadets won 102 of 152 games in Knight's six seasons there. He came to Indiana in 1972, and one year later, the Hoosiers were in the Final Four. Knight and Indiana reached the Final Four three times in the next twelve years and won each time. The championships (1976, 1981, 1987) are what keep Knight coaching at Indiana, but it is the difficult seasons that are instructive.

"Coaching a really good team is the most fun thing possible," Knight says. "Building toward that is very interesting, but not necessarily fun. It requires patience. ... When I stopped by for my dose of patience, there was a long line. I'm not sure I got any at all."

Knight can be intense on the sideline, but his results are indisputable. He has already produced the best record (235–95) in Big Ten history and guided U.S. teams to victory in the Pan-American Games (1979) and the Olympics (1984). There have been times when outside offers have tempted Knight to leave Indiana, but the tradition seems to hold him.

"I think the thing that has happened with basketball here at Indiana University goes way back to the adoption by the people of the state of Indiana and the inception of the state tournament," he says. "I think that people who are really high school basketball fans have attached an allegiance with Indiana. Certainly, in the Midwest we have maintained a far greater statewide interest in our basketball team than perhaps any individual school in the country."

## Denny Crum

He doesn't always receive the attention of, say, a Dean Smith or a Bobby Knight, but Denny Crum is clearly in their league. He learned the art of coaching when he played under Wooden at UCLA. Crum graduated in 1958 and spent three years as a graduate assistant to Wooden before moving on to Pierce Junior College for six seasons as assistant and then head coach. In 1967, Crum rejoined Wooden at UCLA and remained until 1971. In those five seasons, the Bruins won five national championships.

Crum, who was Wooden's best recruiter, obviously took notes while he was there. When Crum was hired by the University of Louisville in 1971, his impact was immediate: The Cardinals produced a 26–5 record. A year later, when Crum's recruiting prowess had begun to improve the level of talent,

Louisville was in the Final Four. They made it there again in 1975 and four more times in the 1980s. Only Smith and Wooden have guided teams to the Final Four more than Crum's six visits. The Cardinals were NCAA champions in 1980, with a record of 33–3, and again in 1986, when the mark was 32–7. Only seven other coaches have won two or more national titles.

Crum's record of consistency is impressive. He was the second-fastest major college coach to win two hundred games and three hundred games, reaching those marks in his ninth and fourteenth seasons. Through 1992, Crum's overall record was 496–183, a winning percentage of 73.0, sixth among active coaches and twenty-second on the all-time list. Under Crum, Louisville has won twenty games or more in seventeen of nineteen seasons. In those nineteen seasons, the Cardinals' average record is 24–8.

**After working under John Wooden at UCLA, Denny Crum created his own empire at Louisville. Through 1991, his Cardinals teams had won 477 games.**

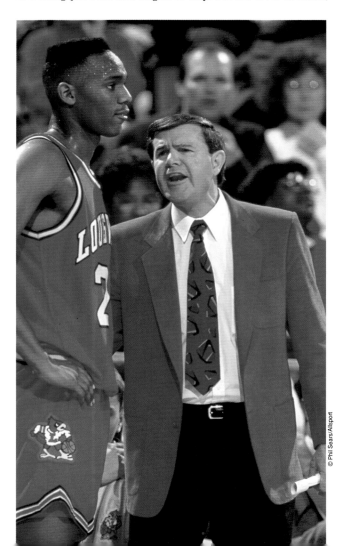

© Phil Sears/Allsport

## John Thompson

In 1964, Red Auerbach thought enough of a six-foot-ten (208-cm), 230-pound (104-kg) Providence University center to make him the Boston Celtics' third-round draft choice. John Thompson played two seasons in Boston, but was, generally, of little consequence. He scored 262 points and grabbed 260 rebounds. At the same time, though, Thompson picked up two NBA championship rings.

Today, as the coach at Georgetown University, he is one of the most dominant coaches in the college game. In nineteen seasons with the Hoyas, Thompson has won 464 games and lost only 165, a winning percentage of 73.8 that places him fifth among active coaches. Thompson had the good fortune to land center Patrick Ewing in 1981, and in three of Ewing's four seasons, Georgetown went to the Final Four. The Hoyas won the 1984 NCAA championship and are a perennial favorite in the rugged Big East Conference.

Thompson has always done things on his own terms. "Nothing's simple," Thompson once said. "Nobody has all the answers. John Thompson's never written a book telling other coaches they should play ten people, sit in the middle of the bench, in the back of the team bus, that they better close their

© Mitchell Layton

**First and last, John Thompson is an educator. His Georgetown players hit the books as often as they hit the court. Oh, and they can play a little basketball, too. His Hoya teams had won 74 percent of their games through 1991.**

practices, keep their freshmen from talking to the press until after January of their first season. See, certain things have worked for me. I tried them and they worked. Which doesn't mean that's the only way. But it's my way. I'm not going to try and force other coaches to change. I did what came naturally to me."

At first glance, Thompson seems destined to place among the biggest winners in NCAA history. But there have been temptations. In 1990, he nearly accepted an $8 million deal from the Denver Nuggets. Thompson has always said getting rich is one of his goals and there are greater possibilities beyond the college level. If he does leave Georgetown, however, the college game will lose one of its best teachers. And that, in the final analysis, is what college coaching is all about.

# THE NCAA TOURNAMENT

It was the shot heard across Connecticut.

The 1990 East Regional semifinal between the University of Connecticut and Clemson University at the raucous Meadowlands in East Rutherford, New Jersey, was all but over. Connecticut, trailing 68–69, had a single second to inbound the ball from under its own net and put up a winning shot at the other end of the court—a long shot at best. Head coach Jim Calhoun told his huddled team they still had a chance to win. "But," said freshman forward Scott Burrell, "I don't know if we believed him."

The plan was for point guard Tate George, the team's only senior, to run a basketball version of a football out-pattern,

into the corner to the right of the Clemson basket. Burrell, a first-round draft choice of the Seattle Mariners as a pitcher, was the obvious choice to produce the pinpoint inbounds heave. "I realized for the first time that my career was coming to an end," George said later. "The guys and the coaches were yelling, 'We've still got time, we've still got time.' But with one second left it's kind of hard to keep that in perspective."

Thus, did Burrell unleash a ninety-four-foot (28.7-m) fast-ball with his powerful pitching arm and, somehow, teammate George caught it cleanly in a crowd of Clemson players. Since no time elapsed until the ball touched George's hand, he had just enough time to spin left, face the basket, and release a sweet seventeen-foot (5.2-m) throw that found nothing but net. It happened just the way Calhoun drew it in the team huddle. In one of the most incredible endings in NCAA Tournament history, Connecticut won 70–69, and a financially troubled state in desperate need of a diversion was captivated.

The dream season ended a day later when Duke University's Christian Laettner produced his own improbable shot, a sixteen-footer (4.9-m) at the buzzer, to give Duke a 79–78 overtime victory over the UConn Huskies. The loss stung momentarily, but in Connecticut, where the state university had never before reached the Final Eight, it was a tremendous breakthrough. For more than a month, nothing else really mattered, which is just one more reason why they call it March Madness. UConn went an unprecedented 31–6, produced a ten-game winning streak, won the Big East Conference for the first time ever, and orchestrated three victories in the tournament. The team was greeted by thousands of fans when it returned to the campus in Storrs.

"I really think the reason people poured out and why we all attached ourselves to this team is that the kids brought back the idea of the word 'teammate'" observed Calhoun, who was named the National Coach of the Year. "What these kids gave each other was teammates. It's not the game or the result that's important. It's the special thing about a group of people."

Said then–athletic director Todd Turner: "Connecticut is a national name today, for maybe some of the wrong reasons, because of a basketball team. All the people in Connecticut, from Tate George to coach Jim Calhoun and Todd Turner and

© Wide World Photos, Inc.

In the 1991 NCAA men's basketball semi-final, UNLV sent Duke guard Bobby Hurley flying.

Governor [William] O'Neill to the guy that sleeps on the street corner have a sense of feeling good about themselves. I think that's the greatest contribution our basketball team has made."

And so, the light went on in Connecticut, just as it did years before in places like North Carolina, Indiana, Louisville, Los Angeles, and Washington, D.C. Beyond the euphoria came the dividends that a winning collegiate program can bring. There was a windfall of $779,917 (less expenses) for appearing in the school's first NCAA Tournament in a decade. The Huskies made several national television appearances the following season for a substantial fee. Donations to athletics and other university concerns increased appreciably. The Huskies enjoyed their finest recruiting effort ever, assembling by most assessments the second-best group in the country. The school also saw applications increase because of the basketball team's national visibility.

Such perquisites were not new for either Duke or the University of Nevada at Las Vegas, also Final Four contenders.

The Duke Blue Devils were no strangers to the annual NCAA Division I Tournament; their advancement to Denver in 1990 was the team's fourth such berth in five years. The Running Rebels of UNLV had reached the Final Four two previous times. Their meeting in the championship game provided a striking contrast.

"Welcome Fellow Scholars," read the sarcastic sign displayed by Duke's Blue Devil mascot. Duke, representing everything good, was coached by Mike Krzyzewski, a man revered for his character and understanding of the role academics plays in college life. The Running Rebels, cast as the bad boys, came from glitzy Las Vegas where NCAA investigators had been investigating coach Jerry Tarkanian for violating NCAA rules.

"Good versus bad?" asked UNLV's Stacey Augmon. "We don't mind what people think of us. The Detroit Pistons were the Bad Boys, too, and look where they ended up." As NBA champions. Twice.

UNLV, also discrediting the good-over-evil expectation, turned a 57–47 second-half lead into a 75–47 advantage with

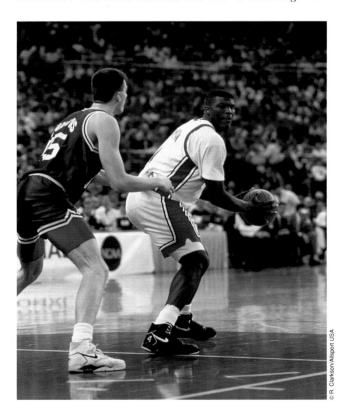

eighteen consecutive points. The final score was 103–73, making it the most one-sided championship game in fifty-two years of the NCAA Tournament. It was the first time a team reached the century mark in scoring. UNLV's Larry Johnson, a six-foot-seven (201-cm), 245-pound (111-kg) force, contributed twenty-two points, eleven rebounds, and four steals, while teammate Anderson Hunt scored twenty-nine points to claim the Final Four's MVP award. "It was scary just watching them. They engulfed us," said Duke center Alaa Abdelnaby.

The outcome was typical of the tournament's first four decades. In the inaugural tournament in 1939, district playoffs were held to determine the eight-team field. Oregon bounced Ohio State in the final, 46–33. A year later, Indiana dusted Kansas 60–42. Soon, the results grew predictable. Henry Iba's Oklahoma State team became the first to repeat as champion, winning in 1945 and 1946. The University of Kentucky, under coach Adolph Rupp, won three of four titles between 1948 and

Dean Smith's North Carolina teams are always in the NCAA hunt.

**In 1985, unheralded Villanova cut down a more talented Georgetown team to win the NCAA crown.**

1951. Bill Russell's University of San Francisco teams of 1955 and 1956 went all the way, and the University of Cincinnati won back-to-back titles in 1961 and 1962 before UCLA changed the NCAA Tournament landscape forever.

Under coach John Wooden and a string of great players like Lew Alcindor, Bill Walton, Marques Johnson, Gail Goodrich, Walt Hazzard, Sidney Wicks, Keith Wilkes, and Dave Meyers, UCLA won ten titles in twelve years, including an unheard of seven in a row. The field had fluctuated between twenty-two and twenty-five teams during that time, but UCLA's final championship came in 1975, the year the tournament was expanded to include thirty-two entries. Further parity visited the NCAA Tournament in the 1980s. The field was expanded to sixty-four schools in 1985, giving all legitimate teams a chance to compete for the national title. The introduction of the forty-five-second clock in 1986 and the arrival of the three-point shot a year later opened up the inside game, and scoring, which hit an all-time low in 1982, rose dramatically. (Interestingly, three of the decade's national champions would not have been invited to compete in the tournament before the expansion to thirty-two teams.) The result was a handful of magnificent games, four of them decided on last-minute shots. They helped the NCAA Tournament join the World Series and Super Bowl as the most eagerly anticipated and talked about sporting events of the year.

One of the most memorable games was in 1982, when a University of North Carolina freshman named Michael Jordan was willing to take the shot that mattered most. He was a skinny nineteen-year-old kid, but the smooth shot and the wagging tongue were already in evidence when the Tar Heels moved through the field and faced Georgetown in the Louisiana Superdome final. In truth, Jordan was not the automatic scorer he is today. He averaged a mere 13.5 points per game for coach Dean Smith's 31–2 number one ranked team. Forward James Worthy and center Sam Perkins provided the bulk of North Carolina's offense, but Georgetown posed some problems. The Hoyas, 30–6, played insufferable defense, anchored by seven-foot (213-cm) freshman center Patrick Ewing. With less than four minutes left, the two superb freshmen met under the Georgetown basket. Jordan soared in for a left-handed layup that just cleared Ewing's enormous wingspan to give the Tar Heels a 61–58 lead. After the Hoyas took a 62–61

lead, Jordan found himself with the ball and a little daylight. He fired a sixteen-foot (4.9-m) shot that gave North Carolina a 63–62 lead with seventeen seconds left. That was the final score. When Georgetown guard Fred Brown inadvertently threw a pass into the arms of Worthy, the game was essentially over. It was a terrific game that introduced the nation to several future NBA draft choices and the wonder of Michael Jordan.

North Carolina, with its dazzling cast and tidy win-loss record, was expected to win the 1982 title. A year later, cross-state rival North Carolina State stunned the basketball world. The Wolfpack scraped into the tournament with ten losses, but no one gave them a second thought. Never before had a team with double-digit losses come away as the champion. But you certainly couldn't deny North Carolina State's chances after its harrowing 69–67 first-round victory over Pepperdine in double-overtime. But Nevada-Las Vegas fell 71–70 in the second round, and Utah followed, 75–56, in the third. Virginia and Georgia were next, and suddenly, Jim Valvano's Wolfpack was staring at the mighty University of Houston in the final. The Cougars, who had shredded a respectable Louisville team 94–81 in the semifinals with an awesome blend of speed and power dunking, were huge favorites in Albuquerque, New Mexico.

The Wolfpack didn't have the thoroughbred athletes to enable them to play above the rim with Houston. Rather, they subsisted on three-point shots from the perimeter. Somehow, North Carolina State pushed out to a 33–25 halftime lead, but Houston countered with a 17–2 run in the first ten minutes of the second half to take a 42–35 lead. Houston coach Guy Lewis called for a slowdown offense and the Wolfpack crept back into the game. Derrick Whittenburg evened the game at fifty-two all with a long three-pointer with just under two minutes to play. With time running down and the score tied, Whittenburg couldn't find an open teammate under the basket, so he launched a ridiculous thirty-foot (9.1-m) shot. It was short, but teammate Lorenzo Charles recognized this before Houston center Hakeem Olajuwon and caught the ball in mid-air, jamming it home for a resounding 54–52 victory.

There was another championship gem in 1985 when Villanova stunned defending champion Georgetown 66–64 in the final. In 1987, Indiana beat Syracuse 74–73 on Keith Smart's sixteen-footer (4.9-m) with five seconds left. It was the same spot on the same floor that Jordan and his teammates had beaten Georgetown five years earlier. And like Jordan, Smart wore number 23. In 1989, University of Michigan's Rumeal Robinson drilled a pair of free throws with three seconds left to beat Seton Hall, 80–79, in the championship game.

The NCAA Tournament is the crucible where a players' greatness can be born or confirmed. Scan the tournament record book and the familiar names jump out. For instance, consider the highlights of the top ten list for most rebounds in two games of a Final Four: Elgin Baylor (41), Lew Alcindor (41), Bill Walton (41), Elvin Hayes (40), Hakeem Olajuwon (40), Artis Gilmore (37), and Oscar Robertson (36). How about the Final Four MVP roster? Among the luminaries are Bill Russell (1955), Wilt Chamberlain (1957), Elgin Baylor (1958), Jerry West (1959), Bill Bradley (1965), Lew Alcindor (1967, 1968, 1969), Bill Walton (1972, 1973), David Thompson (1974), Magic Johnson (1979), Isiah Thomas (1981), James Worthy (1982), Hakeem Olajuwon (1983), Patrick Ewing (1984) and Danny Manning (1988). You could field an NBA All-Star Team with the MVP's of the 1980s alone. Who knows what the 1990s hold?

**This 1984 NCAA Tournament game between Virginia and Houston had the crowd on its feet.**

© R. Mackson/FPG International

**Chris Webber may have cost Michigan the 1993 NCAA championship game by calling a timeout the Wolverines did not have, but his contribution to the professional game may erase that memory.**

## FINAL FOUR SINGLE GAME
## SINGLE GAME, INDIVIDUAL

**Most Points**
58, Bill Bradley, Princeton vs. Wichita St., N3d, 1965
48, Hal Lear, Temple vs. Southern Methodist, N3d, 1956
44, Bill Walton, UCLA vs. Memphis St., CH, 1973
42, Bob Houbregs, Washington vs. Louisiana St., N3d, 1953
42, Jack Egan, St. Joseph's (Pa.) vs. Utah, N3d, 1961
42, Gail Goodrich, UCLA vs. Michigan, CH, 1965
41, Jack Givens, Kentucky vs. Duke, CH, 1978
39, Oscar Robertson, Cincinnati vs. Louisville, N3d, 1959
39, Al Wood, North Caro. vs. Virginia, NSF, 1981
38, Jerry West, West Va. vs. Louisville, NSF, 1959
38, Jerome Chambers, Utah vs. UTEP, NSF, 1966
38, Freddie Banks, Nevada-Las Vegas vs. Indiana, NSF, 1987

© Jonathan Daniel/Allsport USA

## NCAA DIVISION I RECORDS

### CAREER POINTS

| Player, Team | Ht. | Last Year | Yrs. | G | FG | 3FG# | FT | Pts. |
|---|---|---|---|---|---|---|---|---|
| Pete Maravich, Louisiana St. | 6–5 | 1970 | 3 | 83 | 1,387 | — | 893 | 3,667 |
| Freeman Williams, Portland St. | 6–4 | 1978 | 4 | 106 | 1,369 | — | 511 | 3,249 |
| Lionel Simmons, La Salle | 6–8 | 1990 | 4 | 131 | 1,244 | 56 | 673 | 3,217 |
| Harry Kelly, Texas Southern | 6–7 | 1983 | 4 | 110 | 1,234 | — | 598 | 3,066 |
| Hersey Hawkins, Bradley | 6–3 | 1988 | 4 | 125 | 1,100 | 118 | 690 | 3,008 |
| Oscar Robertson, Cincinnati | 6–5 | 1960 | 3 | 88 | 1,052 | — | 869 | 2,973 |
| Danny Manning, Kansas | 6–10 | 1988 | 4 | 147 | 1,216 | 10 | 509 | 2,951 |
| Alfredrick Hughes, Loyola (Ill.) | 6–5 | 1985 | 4 | 120 | 1,226 | — | 462 | 2,914 |
| Elvin Hayes, Houston | 6–8 | 1968 | 3 | 93 | 1,215 | — | 454 | 2,884 |
| Larry Bird, Indiana St. | 6–9 | 1979 | 3 | 94 | 1,154 | — | 542 | 2,850 |

### CAREER ASSISTS

| Player, Team | Ht. | Last Year | Yrs. | G | Ast. |
|---|---|---|---|---|---|
| Chris Corchiani, N.C. State | 6–1 | 1991 | 4 | 124 | 1,038 |
| Keith Jenning, E. Tenn. State | 5–7 | 1991 | 4 | 127 | 983 |
| Sherman Douglas, Syracuse | 6–0 | 1989 | 4 | 138 | 960 |
| Greg Anthony, Portland, UNLV | 6–1 | 1991 | 4 | 138 | 950 |
| Gary Payton, Oregon St. | 6–2 | 1990 | 4 | 120 | 939 |
| Andre LaFleur, Northeastern | 6–3 | 1987 | 4 | 128 | 894 |
| Jim Les, Bradley | 5–11 | 1986 | 4 | 118 | 884 |
| Frank Smith, Old Dominion | 6–0 | 1988 | 4 | 120 | 883 |
| Taurence Chisholm, Delaware | 5–7 | 1988 | 4 | 110 | 877 |
| Grayson Marshall, Clemson | 6–2 | 1988 | 4 | 122 | 857 |
| Anthony Manuel, Bradley | 5–11 | 1989 | 4 | 108 | 855 |
| Avery Johnson, Cameron & Southern-B.R. | 5–11 | 1988 | 3 | 94 | 838 |
| Pooh Richardson, UCLA | 6–1 | 1989 | 4 | 122 | 833 |
| Butch Moore, Southern Methodist | 5–10 | 1986 | 4 | 125 | 828 |
| Drafton Davis, Marist | 6–0 | 1988 | 4 | 115 | 804 |
| Marc Brown, Siena | 5–11 | 1991 | 4 | 123 | 796 |
| Tyrone Bogues, Wake Forest | 5–3 | 1987 | 4 | 119 | 781 |
| Jeff Timberlake, Boston U. | 6–2 | 1989 | 4 | 121 | 778 |
| Kenny Smith, North Caro. | 6–3 | 1987 | 4 | 127 | 768 |
| Bruce Douglas, Illinois | 6–3 | 1986 | 4 | 130 | 765 |
| Andre Turner, Memphis St. | 5–10 | 1986 | 4 | 132 | 763 |
| Howard Evans, Temple | 6–1 | 1988 | 4 | 132 | 748 |
| Carl Golston, Loyola (Ill.) | 5–9 | 1986 | 4 | 118 | 742 |
| Mark Jackson, St. John's (N.Y.) | 6–2 | 1987 | 4 | 131 | 738 |

### CAREER REBOUNDS
#### For Careers Beginning in 1973 or After

| Player, Team | Ht. | Last Year | Yrs. | G | Reb. |
|---|---|---|---|---|---|
| Ralph Sampson, Virginia | 7–4 | 1983 | 4 | 132 | 1,511 |
| Pete Padgett, Nevada-Reno | 6–8 | 1976 | 4 | 104 | 1,464 |
| Michael Brooks, La Salle | 6–7 | 1980 | 4 | 114 | 1,372 |
| Xavier McDaniel, Wichita St. | 6–7 | 1985 | 4 | 117 | 1,359 |
| John Irving, Hofstra | 6–9 | 1977 | 4 | 103 | 1,348 |
| Sam Clancy, Pittsburgh | 6–6 | 1981 | 4 | 116 | 1,342 |
| Keith Lee, Memphis St. | 6–10 | 1985 | 4 | 128 | 1,336 |
| Larry Smith, Alcorn St. | 6–8 | 1980 | 4 | 111 | 1,334 |
| Michael Cage, San Diego St. | 6–9 | 1984 | 4 | 112 | 1,217 |
| Bob Stephens, Drexel | 6–7 | 1979 | 4 | 99 | 1,316 |

# BASKETBALL HALL OF FAME ELECTEES

## Players

| | |
|---|---|
| Archibald, Nate | 1990 |
| Arizin, Paul J. | 1977 |
| Barlow, Thomas | 1980 |
| Baylor, Elgin | 1976 |
| Beckman, John | 1972 |
| Borgmann, Bennie | 1961 |
| Bradley, William | 1982 |
| Brennan, Joseph | 1974 |
| Cervi, Alfred N. | 1984 |
| Chamberlain, Wilt | 1978 |
| Cooper, Charles (Tarzan) | 1976 |
| Cousy, Robert J. | 1970 |
| Cowens, Dave | 1990 |
| Cunningham, William J. | 1985 |
| Davies, Robert E. | 1969 |
| DeBernardi, Forrest S. | 1961 |
| DeBusschere, Dave | 1982 |
| Dehnert, Henry G. | 1968 |
| Endacott, Paul | 1971 |
| Foster, Harold (Bud) | 1964 |
| Friedman, Max (Marty) | 1971 |
| Fulks, Joseph F. | 1977 |
| Gale, Lauren (Laddie) | 1976 |
| Gallatin, Harry | 1990 |
| Gola, Thomas J. | 1975 |
| Greer, Harold | 1981 |
| Gruenig, Robert | 1963 |
| Hagan, Clifford O. | 1977 |
| Hanson, Victor | 1960 |
| Havlicek, John J. | 1983 |
| Heinsohn, Thomas W. | 1985 |
| Holman, Nat | 1964 |
| Hyatt, Charles (Chuck) | 1959 |
| Johnson, William C. | 1976 |
| Jones, Samuel (Sam) | 1983 |
| Krause, Edward W. | 1975 |
| Kurland, Robert A. | 1961 |
| Lapchick, Joseph | 1966 |
| Lucas, Jerry Ray | 1979 |
| Luisetti, Angelo (Hank) | 1959 |
| McCracken, Branch | 1960 |
| McCracken, Jack | 1962 |
| Macauley, Edward C. | 1960 |
| Martin, Slater | 1981 |
| Mikan, George L. | 1959 |
| Murphy, Charles (Stretch) | 1960 |
| Page, Harlan O. | 1962 |
| Pettit, Robert L. | 1970 |
| Phillip, Andy | 1961 |
| Pollard, James C. | 1977 |
| Ramsey, Frank | 1981 |
| Reed, Willis | 1981 |
| Robertson, Oscar | 1979 |
| Roosma, Col. John S. | 1961 |
| Russell, John (Honey) | 1964 |
| Russell, William F. | 1974 |

| | |
|---|---|
| Schayes, Adolph | 1972 |
| Schmidt, Ernest J. | 1973 |
| Schommer, John J. | 1959 |
| Sedran, Barney | 1962 |
| Sharman, William W. | 1975 |
| Steinmetz, Christian | 1961 |
| Thompson, John A. | 1962 |
| Thurmond, Nate | 1984 |
| Twyman, Jack | 1982 |
| Vandivier, Robert (Fuzzy) | 1974 |
| Wachter, Edward A. | 1961 |
| West, Jerry Alan | 1979 |
| Wooden, John R. | 1960 |

## Coaches

| | |
|---|---|
| Anderson, W. Harold | 1984 |
| Auerbach, Arnold J. (Red) | 1968 |
| Barry, Justin (Sam) | 1978 |
| Blood, Ernest A. | 1960 |
| Cann, Howard G. | 1967 |
| Carlson, Dr. H. Clifford | 1959 |
| Carnevale, Ben | 1969 |
| Case, Everett | 1981 |
| Dean, Everett S. | 1966 |
| Diddle, Edgar A. | 1971 |
| Drake, Bruce | 1972 |
| Gaines, Clarence | 1981 |
| Gardner, James H. (Jack) | 1983 |
| Gill, Amory T. | 1967 |
| Harshman, Marv | 1984 |
| Hickey, Edgar S. (Eddie) | 1978 |
| Hobson, Howard A. | 1965 |
| Holzman, William (Red) | 1985 |
| Iba, Henry P. | 1968 |
| Julian, Alvin F. | 1967 |
| Keaney, Frank W. | 1960 |
| Keogan, George E. | 1961 |
| Knight, Bob | 1990 |
| Lambert, Ward L. | 1960 |
| Litwack, Harry | 1975 |
| Leoffler, Kenneth D. | 1964 |
| Lonborg, Arthur C. | 1972 |
| McCutchan, Arad A. | 1980 |
| McGuire, Frank J. | 1976 |
| Meanwell, Dr. Walter E. | 1959 |
| Meyer, Raymond J. | 1978 |
| Rupp, Adolph F. | 1968 |
| Sachs, Leonard D. | 1961 |
| Shelton, Everett F. | 1979 |
| Smith, Dean | 1982 |
| Taylor, Fred R. | 1985 |
| Wade, L. Margaret | 1984 |
| Watts, Stanley H. | 1985 |
| Wooden, John R. | 1972 |

# NBA WORLD CHAMPIONSHIPS BY FRANCHISE

| Team | Number | Last | Coach |
|---|---|---|---|
| Boston Celtics | 16 | 1985–86 | K. C. Jones |
| Minneapolis-Los Angeles Lakers | 11 | 1987–88 | Pat Riley |
| Philadelphia-Golden State Warriors | 3 | 1974–75 | Al Attles |
| Syracuse Nats-Philadelphia 76ers | 3 | 1982–83 | Billy Cunningham |
| Chicago Bulls | 3 | 1992–93 | Phil Jackson |
| New York Knickerbockers | 2 | 1972–73 | Red Holzman |
| Detroit Pistons | 2 | 1989–90 | Chuck Daly |
| Baltimore Bullets* | 1 | 1947–48 | Buddy Jeannette |
| Milwaukee Bucks | 1 | 1970–71 | Larry Costello |
| Portland Trail Blazers | 1 | 1976–77 | Jack Ramsay |
| Rochester Royals-Sacramento Kings | 1 | 1950–51 | Lester Harrison |
| St. Louis-Atlanta Hawks | 1 | 1957–58 | Alex Hannum |
| Seattle SuperSonics | 1 | 1978–79 | Lenny Wilkens |
| Washington Bullets | 1 | 1977–78 | Dick Motta |

*Defunct

## TOP TEN PERFORMANCES IN PLAYOFFS
### Most Points Scored in One Game

| | FG. | FT. | Pts. |
|---|---|---|---|
| Michael Jordan, Chicago at Boston, April 20, 1986 ....** | 22 | 19 | 63 |
| Elgin Baylor, Los Angeles at Boston, April 14, 1962 ...... | 22 | 17 | 61 |
| Wilt Chamberlain, Philadelphia vs. Syracuse at Philadelphia, March 22, 1962 ..................... | 22 | 12 | 56 |
| Rick Barry, San Francisco vs. Philadelphia at San Francisco, April 18, 1967 ...................... | 22 | 11 | 55 |
| Michael Jordan, Chicago vs. Cleveland, May 1, 1988 ... | 24 | 7 | 55 |
| John Havlicek, Boston vs. Atlanta at Boston, April 1, 1973 ...................... | 24 | 6 | 54 |
| Wilt Chamberlain, Philadelphia vs. Syracuse at Philadelphia, March 14, 1960 .................... | 24 | 5 | 53 |
| Jerry West, Los Angeles vs. Boston, April 23, 1969 ..... | 21 | 11 | 53 |
| Jerry West, Los Angeles vs. Baltimore at Los Angeles, April 5, 1965 ...................... | 16 | 20 | 52 |
| Sam Jones, Boston at New York, March 30, 1967 ....... | 19 | 13 | 51 |

*Denotes each overtime period played.

## RESULTS OF ALL-STAR GAMES

| Year | Result and Locations | Most Valuable Player |
|---|---|---|
| 1951 | East 111, West 94 at Boston | Ed Macauley, Boston |
| 1952 | East 108, West 91 at Boston | Paul Arizin, Philadelphia |
| 1953 | West 79, East 75 at Fort Wayne | George Mikan, Minnesota |
| 1954 | East 98, West 93 (OT) at New York | Bob Cousy, Boston |
| 1955 | East 100, West 91 at New York | Bill Sharman, Boston |
| 1956 | West 108, East 94 at Rochester | Bob Pettit, St. Louis |
| 1957 | East 109, West 97 at Boston | Bob Cousy, Boston |
| 1958 | East 130, West 118 at St. Louis | Bob Pettit, St. Louis |
| 1959 | West 124, East 108 at Detroit | E. Baylor, Mn. & B. Pettit, St.L. |
| 1960 | East 125, West 115 at Philadelphia | Wilt Chamberlain, Philadelphia |
| 1961 | West 153, East 131 at Syracuse | Oscar Robertson, Cincinnati |
| 1962 | West 150, East 130 at St. Louis | Bob Pettit, St. Louis |
| 1963 | East 115, West 108 at Los Angeles | Bill Russell, Boston |
| 1964 | East 111, West 107 at Boston | Oscar Robertson, Cincinnati |
| 1965 | East 124, West 123 at St. Louis | Jerry Lucas, Cincinnati |
| 1966 | East 137, West 94 at Cincinnati | Adrian Smith, Cincinnati |
| 1967 | West 135, East 120 at San Francisco | Rick Barry, San Francisco |
| 1968 | East 144, West 124 at New York | Hal Greer, Philadelphia |
| 1969 | East 123, West 112 at Baltimore | Oscar Robertson, Cincinnati |
| 1970 | East 142, West 135 at Philadelphia | Willis Reed, New York |
| 1971 | West 108, East 107 at San Diego | Len Wilkens, Seattle |
| 1972 | West 112, East 110 at Los Angeles | Jerry West, Los Angeles |
| 1973 | East 104, West 84 at Chicago | Dave Cowens, Boston |
| 1974 | West 134, East 123 at Seattle | Bob Lanier, Detroit |
| 1975 | East 108, West 102 at Phoenix | Walt Frazier, New York |
| 1976 | East 123, West 109 at Philadelphia | Dave Bing, Washington |
| 1977 | West 125, East 124 at Milwaukee | Julius Erving, Philadelphia |
| 1978 | East 133, West 125 at Atlanta | Randy Smith, Buffalo |
| 1979 | West 134, East 129 at Detroit | David Thompson, Denver |
| 1980 | East 144, West 135 (OT) at Landover | George Gervin, San Antonio |
| 1981 | East 123, West 120 at Cleveland | Nate Archibald, Boston |
| 1982 | East 120, West 118 at E. Rutherford | Larry Bird, Boston |
| 1983 | East 132, West 123 at Los Angeles | Julius Erving, Philadelphia |
| 1984 | East 154, West 145 (OT) at Denver | Isiah Thomas, Detroit |
| 1985 | West 140, East 129 at Indianapolis | Ralph Sampson, Houston |
| 1986 | East 139, West 132 at Dallas | Isiah Thomas, Detroit |
| 1987 | West 154, East 149 (OT) at Seattle | Tom Chambers, Seattle |
| 1988 | East 138, West 133 at Chicago | Michael Jordan, Chicago |
| 1989 | West 143, East 134 at Houston | Karl Malone, Utah |
| 1990 | East 130, West 113 at Miami | Magic Johnson, L.A. Lakers |
| 1991 | East 116, West 114 at Charlotte | Charles Barkley, Philadelphia |
| 1992 | West 153, East 113 at Orlando | Magic Johnson, L.A. Lakers |
| 1993 | West 135, East 132 (OT) at Salt Lake City | J. Stockton & K. Malone, Utah |

## ALL-TIME WINNINGEST NBA COACHES

| Coach | W–L | Pct. |
|---|---|---|
| Red Auerbach | 938–479 | .662 |
| Lenny Wilkens | 869–749 | .537 |
| Jack Ramsay | 864–783 | .525 |
| Dick Motta | 849–845 | .501 |
| Bill Fitch | 805–835 | .491 |
| Gene Shue | 784–861 | .477 |
| Don Nelson | 753–541 | .582 |
| Cotton Fitzsimmons | 752–716 | .512 |
| John MacLeod | 707–657 | .518 |
| Red Holzman | 696–604 | .535 |
| Pat Riley | 644–247 | .723 |
| Doug Moe | 609–492 | .553 |
| Al Attles | 557–518 | .518 |
| Chuck Daly | 519–342 | .603 |
| K. C. Jones | 504–234 | .683 |
| Alex Hannum | 471–412 | .533 |
| Billy Cunningham | 454–196 | .698 |
| Larry Costello | 430–300 | .589 |
| Tom Heinsohn | 427–263 | .619 |
| John Kundla | 423–302 | .583 |
| Larry Brown | 349–272 | .562 |
| Bill Russell | 341–290 | .540 |
| Hubie Brown | 341–410 | .454 |
| Kevin Loughery | 341–503 | .404 |
| Bill Sharman | 333–240 | .581 |
| Richie Guerin | 327–291 | .529 |
| Al Cervi | 326–241 | .575 |
| Joe Lapchick | 326–247 | .569 |
| Mike Fratello | 324–253 | .562 |
| Del Harris | 324–332 | .494 |
| Fred Schaus | 315–245 | .563 |
| Stan Albeck | 307–267 | .535 |
| Lester Harrison | 295–181 | .620 |
| Frank Layden | 277–294 | .485 |
| Paul Seymour | 271–241 | .529 |
| Bill Van Breda Kolff | 266–255 | .511 |
| Eddie Gottlieb | 263–318 | .453 |
| Jack McMahon | 260–289 | .474 |
| Tom Nissalke | 248–391 | .388 |
| Jerry Sloan | 243–201 | .547 |
| Phil Johnson | 236–306 | .435 |
| Jim Lynam | 211–217 | .493 |
| Bernie Bickerstaff | 202–208 | .493 |
| Dick McGuire | 197–260 | .431 |
| Don Chaney | 191–240 | .443 |
| Bob Leonard | 186–264 | .413 |
| Matt Guokas | 168–203 | .453 |
| Paul Westhead | 159–166 | .489 |
| Mike Schuler | 158–135 | .539 |
| Dolph Schayes | 151–172 | .467 |
| Ray Scott | 147–134 | .523 |
| Jerry West | 145–101 | .589 |
| Charles Wolf | 143–187 | .433 |
| Bob Cousy | 141–209 | .403 |
| Doug Collins | 137–109 | .557 |
| Rick Adelman | 136– 63 | .683 |
| Harry Gallatin | 136–120 | .531 |
| Buddy Jeannette | 136–173 | .440 |
| Jack McKinney | 136–215 | .387 |
| Wes Unseld | 131–170 | .435 |
| Johnny Egan | 129–152 | .459 |
| Charlie Eckman | 123–118 | .510 |
| Paul Birch | 120–147 | .449 |

# SELECTED MEMORABLE EVENTS IN BASKETBALL HISTORY

*(Courtesy of the Basketball Hall of Fame)*

**December 1891:** Dr. James Naismith, an instructor at the School for Christian Workers in Springfield, Massachusetts, invents the game of basket ball (then two words).

**March 11, 1892:** Students and teachers at the School for Christian Workers play the first public game of basket ball. Before a crowd of 200, the students win, 5–1. Amos Alonzo Stagg averts a shutout by scoring the teachers' only goal.

**March 22, 1893:** Smith College in Northampton, Massachusetts, becomes the first women's school to play basket ball. Men are not permitted to watch the games.

**1894:** The free throw line is moved to 15 feet (4.6 m) from 20 feet (6.1 m).

**1895:** The field goal value is changed to two points from three points. Foul shots are reduced from three points to one point.

**1896:** The first professional basket ball game is reportedly played at the Masonic Temple Auditorium in Trenton, New Jersey.

**1904:** Columbia University claims the mythical national title by beating Minnesota (27–15) and Wisconsin (21–15) during the regular season.

**1907:** The Buffalo Germans begin a streak of 111 consecutive victories that will carry into 1910.

**1909:** Players committing a fourth personal foul are now disqualified from the game.

**1913:** The opponent of the last player to touch the ball before it goes out of bounds is awarded a throw-in.

**1921:** Copy editors, take note. Basket ball becomes basketball.

**1923:** Passaic High School (New Jersey) sets a national record for boys with 159 consecutive victories.

**February 25, 1924:** Marie Boyd scores 156 points for Lonaconing Central (Maryland) in a 162–3 victory over Cumberland Ursuline Academy (Maryland). This is not a misprint. It is, not surprisingly, a national record for girls.

**1931:** A tournament in Peking, China, attracts 70,000 fans over three nights.

**December 29, 1934:** Promoter Ned Irish produces the first college basketball doubleheader at New York's Madison Square Garden. New York University defeats Notre Dame 25–18, and Westminster beats St. John's 37–33 with 16,188 in the seats.

**August 1–16, 1936:** Basketball becomes an official Olympic sport. The United States defeats Canada, 19–8, for the gold medal in Berlin.

**December 30, 1936:** Hank Luisetti's one-hand set shot becomes the rage when his Stanford team ends Long Island University's forty-three-game winning streak. Until this point, everyone had used the classic two-hand shot.

**February 28, 1940:** Basketball goes big-time. A Madison Square Garden doubleheader featuring Pittsburgh and Fordham (57–37), and New York University and Georgetown (50–27) involves the first basketball games ever televised.

**1943:** Height makes right. Bob Kurland, a legitimate seven-footer (213-cm), enrolls at Oklahoma, and six-foot-ten (207-cm) George Mikan arrives at DePaul. They are the first big men to dominate play.

**June 6, 1946:** The Basketball Association of America, the forerunner of today's NBA, is founded. Future Hall of Famer Maurice Podoloff is the first president.

**November 1, 1946:** The New York Knicks' Ossie Schectman becomes the first player to score a field goal in the fledgling league. He scores on a lay-up after a feed from teammate Leo Gottlieb, and the Knicks go on to beat the Toronto Huskies, 68–66.

**1950:** Duquesne University's Charles Cooper becomes the first black man drafted by an NBA team, the Boston Celtics.

**November 22, 1950:** The Fort Wayne Pistons defeat the Minneapolis Lakers, 19–18, in the lowest-scoring game in NBA history. The loss ends a twenty-nine-game winning streak at home for the Lakers. George Mikan scores fifteen of his team's eighteen points.

**1951:** A crowd of 75,000 people, a record for a basketball game, watch the Harlem Globetrotters perform at Berlin's Olympic Stadium.

**January 6, 1951:** Indianapolis edges Rochester 75–73 in six overtime periods, the NBA's longest game ever.

**1952:** The foul lane is widened to twelve feet (3.7 m) from six feet (1.8 m).

**October 30, 1954:** The twenty-four-second clock is used for the first time in an NBA game. The results are immediate; the game quickens. Rochester defeats Boston, 98–95.

**March 23, 1957:** North Carolina posts a perfect 32–0 record to win the NCAA championship. Frank McGuire's Tar Heels survive six overtime periods at Kansas City's Municipal Auditorium, three in the final to outlast Wilt Chamberlain's Kansas team, 54–53.

**1958:** Oscar Robertson becomes the first sophomore in history to win the NCAA scoring title. He averages an astounding 35.1 points per game for Cincinnati.

**January 26, 1960:** (Aptly named) Danny Heater of (aptly named) Burnsville High School (West Virginia) scores 135 points in a thirty-two-minute game as Burnsville defeats Widen High School, 173–43. Heater sinks fifty-three of seventy field goals, twenty-nine of forty-one free throws, and adds thirty-two rebounds.

**1960:** The Minneapolis Lakers move to Los Angeles, giving professional basketball its first coast-to-coast presence.

**1963:** Players assessed with a personal foul must now raise their arm to acknowledge the transgression.

**January 29, 1964:** Boone Trail High School of Mamers (North Carolina) survives Angier High School (North Carolina) 56–54 in thirteen overtimes, a record for the longest scholastic game ever played.

**1967:** Prohibition lives. The slam dunk is banned in intercollegiate play.

**November 19, 1967:** Jerry Harkness of the Indiana Pacers tosses in a ninety-two-foot (28-m) field goal against the Dallas Chapparalls for a professional distance record.

**January 20, 1968:** A Houston Astrodome crowd of 52,693 watches Elvin Hayes score thirty-nine points to help Houston break UCLA's forty-seven-game winning streak, 71–69. In terms of national exposure, it is college basketball's watershed event.

**February, 1971:** Women are granted equal rights on the basketball court; now five women play on a side, compared to the previous total of six.

**January 9, 1972:** The Milwaukee Bucks defeat the Los Angeles Lakers 120–104, ending the Lakers' professional sports record of thirty-three consecutive victories.

**1972:** Freshmen are now allowed to play on collegiate varsity teams.

**September 9, 1972:** The United States loses its first Olympic basketball game since teams began competing in 1936. The USSR is awarded a 51–50 victory on a disputed call, ending the USA's sixty-three-game winning streak.

**March 25, 1974:** North Carolina State wins the NCAA title, upsetting UCLA 80–77 in double overtime of the semifinal and Marquette (76–64) in the final. That ends UCLA's record of seven consecutive titles and thirty-eight victories.

**1976:** Hey, we were only kidding. The slam dunk is legal again in college basketball.

**1976:** Women's basketball, finally, becomes a full-fledged Olympic event in Montreal. The USSR beats the United States 112–77 in the gold medal final.

**1979:** The NBA adopts the three-point field goal. It also eliminates the third referee.

**September 5, 1979:** Ann Meyers, a four-time All-America at UCLA, becomes the first woman to sign an NBA contract. She fails to make the Indiana Pacers team.

**December 21, 1980:** UCLA defeats Temple 73–49 at Yoyogi Gym in Tokyo, in the first sanctioned NCAA game ever played in a foreign nation.

**July 29, 1982:** The University of San Francisco, former national champions (1955 and 1956), drops its men's basketball program.

**April 1, 1983:** President Ronald Reagan sends $10,000 worth of basketball equipment to Burundi, one of the world's smallest and poorest nations. Answering cynics who say the move was pure public relations, White House officials insist the date is a coincidence.

**December 13, 1983:** The Detroit Pistons beat the Denver Nuggets 186–184 in three overtimes, setting single-game records for the most points by both an individual team and in a complete game.

**January 11, 1984:** The Denver Nuggets defeat the San Antonio Spurs 163–155—without overtime! It is the highest-scoring regulation game in NBA history.

**April 5, 1984:** Kareem Abdul-Jabbar of the Los Angeles Lakers sinks a skyhook against the Utah Jazz and surpasses Wilt Chamberlain's career total of 31,419 points to become the NBA's all-time leading scorer.

**November 17, 1984:** Kansas Newman College wins two games in eight hours. Baker University was defeated on the Wichita school's home court in the afternoon, and later, Newman traveled to Hillsboro, Kansas, to beat Tabor 90–79.

**December 21, 1984:** Georgeann Wells of West Virginia becomes the first woman to slam-dunk in collegiate competition.

**1985:** The NCAA approves the use of the forty-five-second clock.

**November 13, 1985:** Lynette Woodward makes her debut with the Harlem Globetrotters in Spokane, Washington. She is the first woman to perform with the 'Trotters.

**June 10, 1986:** Nancy Lieberman suits up and plays for the Springfield Fame of the United States Basketball League, becoming the first woman to play in an organized professional men's basketball league.

**1986:** The NCAA approves a three-point line for men's teams, at nineteen feet, nine inches (6 m).

**January 14, 1987:** John Mills School (Illinois) defeats Giles Elementary School 24–22, ending Giles' five-year, 221-game winning streak.

**February 16, 1987:** Lynne Lorenzen of Ventura High School (Iowa) scores fifty-four points to push her career total to 6,266 points. She finishes her high school career with 6,736 points.

**June 22, 1987:** Three members of Baltimore's Dunbar High School are drafted in the first round of the NBA draft: Reggie Williams (Georgetown and the Los Angeles Clippers), Tyrone Bogues (Wake Forest and the Washington Bullets), and Reggie Lewis (Northeastern and the Boston Celtics).

**January 25, 1988:** Ricky Green of the Utah Jazz scores the NBA's five-millionth point as the Jazz beats the Cleveland Cavaliers 119–96 in Salt Lake City.

**1988:** The NBA returns to the use of a third official.

**January 31, 1989:** Loyola Marymount incinerates U.S. International, 181–150, setting an NCAA record for points scored for two teams and one team.

**March 13, 1989:** The space shuttle *Discovery* carries an official Spalding Hall of Fame red, white, and blue basketball over two million miles. Two months later, astronaut Col. Robert Springer presents the ball to the Hall of Fame.

**November 3, 1989:** Russians Alexander Volkov (Atlanta Hawks) and Sarunas Marciulionis (Golden State) make their NBA debuts.

**January 24, 1990:** Clarence "Big House" Gaines becomes the second collegiate coach to win 800 games. His Winston-Salem team defeats Livingstone, 79–69. Only Kentucky's Adolph Rupp won more games (875).

**February 7, 1990:** Lisa Leslie of Morningside High School (California) scores 101 points against South Torrance High School. With the score 102–24, South Torrance walks off the court in protest.

**February 23, 1991:** The University of North Carolina becomes the first collegiate team to surpass 1,500 victories. The Tar Heels defeat Clemson, 73–57.

**April 19, 1991:** Atlanta's Moses Malone sets the NBA record by playing in the most consecutive games (1,046) without fouling out, breaking Wilt Chamberlain's record.

**January 13, 1992:** The 200-point barrier is broken for the first time in collegiate history. Troy State (Alabama) defeats DeVry Institute, 258–141.

**March 23, 1992:** A second-quarter layup by Atlanta rookie Stacey Augmon is the six-millionth point in NBA history.

**April 14, 1993:** The NCAA announces that the college shot clock will go from 45 seconds to 35 seconds effective for the 1993–94 season.

**April 25, 1993:** Minnesota's Michael Williams breaks Calvin Murphy's 12-year record by sinking 84 consecutive free throws.

# INDEX

## A

Abdelnaby, Alaa, 116
Abdul-Jabbar, Kareem, 14, 27, 30, 64–65, *66*,
    85–86, *86*
    Most Valuable Player, 38
    NBA All-Star Games, 96
    rebounds, 22
    *See also* Alcindor, Lew.
Adams, Michael (Denver Nuggets), *37*, 96
Adelman, Rick (coach), 60
Ainge, Danny (Portland Trail Blazers), *64*
Albany Patroons, 96
Alcindor, Lew, 103, 105, 118
    *See also* Abdul-Jabbar, Kareem.
All-America Team, 103, 108
All-Nigeria Sports Festival, 71
Allen, F.C. "Phog" (coach), 106, 107
American Basketball Association (ABA), 19,
    51, 77, 84
Anejo Rum (Philippines), 96
Archibald, Nate, 41
Assist, the, 26, 28, 40–41
Atlanta Hawks, 12, 28, 31, 54, 104
Attendance figures, 13–14
Auerbach, Arnold "Red," 51, 54, 64, 83,
    86–88, *87*, 91, 94
Augmon, Stacey, 116

## B

Bailey, Damon (Bedford-North Lawrence
    Stars), 10, *10*
Baker University, 107
Barkley, Charles (Phoenix Suns), 14, 34, *34*,
    *36*, 58–60, *61*
Barlow, Ken, 13
Barry, Rick, 28, 77, 95
Bartow, Gene (coach), 105
Basketball
    attendance figures, 13–14
    development of, 19, 21
    internationalization of, 11–12
    origin of, 11, 17–19
    salaries in, 13
Basketball Hall of Fame (Springfield,
    Massachusetts), 27, *27*, 76, 100, 107,
    109
Baylor, Elgin, 21, 79–80, 91, 94
Bee, Clair (coach), 91, 106, 108
Biasone, Danny (owner, Syracuse), 19
Bird, Larry Joe (Boston Celtics), 11, 13, 14,
    *20*, 34, *34*, 51, 54, *55*, 88, *92–93*

free throws, 28
    Most Valuable Player, 38
    NBA All-Star Games, 95
Blocked shot, the, 64
Bogues, Tyrone "Muggsy," 30–31, *30*
Bol, Manute, 30–31, *31*, *70*
Boston Celtics, 11, 13, 19, 51, 54, 60, 62, 64,
    76, 77, 83, 87–88, 91, 96, 104
    NBA championship series, 91, 94, 95
Boston College, 90
Bowie, Sam, 60
Bradley, Bill, 27, 101–102, *102*, 105
Bradley Center (Milwaukee), 106
Bradley, Shawn (Philadelphia 76ers), *34*, *75*
Bridgeman, Junior, 86
Bridgeport University, 31
Brown, Dee (Boston Celtics), 95
Brown, Fred "Downtown," 21
Brown, Larry (coach), 70, 105
Brown, Walter, 77, 87
Burrell, Scott, 114, 115

## C

Calhoun, Jim (coach), 40, 114
Campbell, Tony, 96
Capital Bullets, 60
Carr, Austin, 100, 102, 104, 105
Cartwright, Bill (New York Knicks), 62
CBS Sports, 13, 14
Center
    Abdul-Jabbar, Kareem, 14, 27, 30, 64–65,
        *66*, 85–86, *86*
    Chamberlain, Wilt, 19, 21, 22, 30, 35, 38,
        62, 64, 80, *81*, 94, 96
    decline of, 65
    definition, 37
    Ewing, Patrick, 13, 27, 62, *63*, 65, 71–72,
        112, 118
    Mikan, George, 62, 76–77, *76*, 91
    Olajuwon, Hakeem, 14, 47, 65, *69*, 70–71,
        119
    Robinson, David, 14, *29*, 34, 42, 65, 68, *68*,
        70
    Russell, Bill, 22, 38, 62, 64, 76, 79, *78*, 88,
        91, 94
Central Missouri State University, 107
Chamberlain, Wilt (Philadelphia 76ers), 14,
    19, 21, 35, 62, 64, 80, *81*, 94
    Most Valuable Player, 38, 64
    NBA All-Star Games, 96
    rebounds, 22
    slam dunk, 30
Chambers, Tom (Phoenix Suns), 11–12, 56, 96

Chaney, Don, 103
Charles, Lorenzo, 119
Charlotte Coliseum, 95
Chicago American Gears, 76
Chicago Bears, 14
Chicago Bulls, 13, 46, 58, 91
Chicago Stags, 77
Cincinnati Royals, 94, 101
Clemson University, 114
Cleveland Cavaliers, 13, 90, 104
Coaches, college, 106–112, 114
    Allen, F.C. "Phog," 106, 107
    Crum, Denny, 106, 112, *112*
    Knight, Bobby, 41, 58, 106, 110–111, *111*
    Meyer, Ray, 76, 106, 108
    Rupp, Adolph, 91, 106, 107–108, *108*
    Smith, Dean, 106, 110, 117
    Thompson, John, 34, 72, 106, 112, *113*, 114
    Wooden, John, 10, 14, 30, 103, 105, 109–110,
        *109*, 118
Coaches, professional, 86–91
    Adelman, Rick, 60
    Auerbach, Red, 51, 54, 64, 83, 86–88, *87*, 91
    Brown, Larry, 70
    Collins, Doug, 46
    Cunningham, Billy, 90
    Daly, Chuck, 34, 86, 90–91, *90*
    Harris, Del, 86
    Kundlas, John, 91
    Loughery, Kevin, 51
    Lyman, Jim, 59
    Nelson, Don, 58, 65
    Riley, Pat, 38, 86, 88, *89*
    Westhead, Paul, 88
Colangelo, Jerry (Phoenix Suns), 12
Collegiate basketball, 100–119
    Alcindor, Lew, 103, 105
    Bradley, Bill, 101–102, *102*, 105
    Carr, Austin, 104, 105
    growth of, 14
    Hayes, Elvin, 103, 105
    Manning, Danny, 105–106, *106*
    Maravich, Pete, 103–104, *104*
    NCAA Tournament, 114–116, 118–119
    Robertson, Oscar, 100–101
    Walton, Bill, 105
    West, Jerry, 105
Collins, Doug (coach), 46
Comegys, Dallas, 12
Continental Basketball Association (CBA), 96
Cousy, Bob (Boston Celtics), 27, 28, 40, 70,
    77, 80, 86, 91
    NBA All-Star Games, 96
Cowens, Dave (Boston Celtics), 88
Crum, Denny (coach), 106, 112, *112*
Cunningham, Billy (coach), 90
Cureton, Earl, 112

## D

Daly, Chuck (coach), 34, 86, 90–91, *90*
Dantley, Adrian, 58
Dawkins, Darryl (Philadelphia 76ers), 12, 38
Denver Nuggets, 114
DePaul University, 62, 76, 106, 108
Detroit Pistons, 34, 47, 49, 90, 116
    NBA championship series, 91, 95
Diddle, Ed, 108
Divac, Vlade (Los Angeles Lakers), 12
Dream Team, 34, *34*
Drexler, Clyde "The Glide" (Portland Trail
    Blazers), 47, 48, *52*, 60, *97*
Duckworth, Kevin (Portland Trail Blazers),
    47, 60
Duke University, 90, 115, 116
Dumars III, Joe (Detroit Pistons), 47, 49, *49*

## E

Eastern Conference All-Stars, 50, 51
Eaton, Mark (Utah Jazz), 11, 31, 72, *73*
Edwards, Jay (Marion Giants), *10*
English, Alex (Denver Nuggets), 57
Erving, Julius, 14 *17*, *21*, 47, 51, 77, 84–85, *84*
    NBA All-Star Games, 95, 96
Ewing, Patrick (New York Knicks), 14, 27, 34,
    *34*, 62, *63*, 65, 71–72, 112, 118
Expansion franchises, 14

## F

Ferry, Danny, 12
Final Four (college basketball), *98*
Finesse forward. *See* Small forward.
Floyd, Darrell, 100
Forty-five-second clock (college basketball),
    21, 118
Franklin High School (Indiana), 10
Frazier, Walt, Jr., 12
Fredrick, Zam, 100
Free throw, the, 28, 54
Fulks, Joe, 76
Furman University, 100

## G

Gaines, Clarence "Big House" (coach), 107
Gamble, Kevin, 96

Gaze, Andrew, 12
George, Tate, 114, 115
Georgetown University, 65, 72, 99, 106, 112, 114, 118, 119
Gervin, Derrick, 96
Gervin, George, 12, 95, 96
Gilmore, Artis, 28, 30
Goaltending rule, 62
Golden State Warriors, 12, 31, 42, 58
    NBA championship series, 94
Goodrich, Gail (Los Angeles Lakers), 91, 110, 118
Grant, Horace (Chicago Bulls), 59
Green, Bill (high school coach), 9–11, 9

**H**

Hagan, Cliff, 88
Hardaway, Tim (Golden State Warriors), 42
Harlem Globetrotters, 35, 35, 62, 80
Harper, Ron (Cleveland Cavaliers), 49–50
Harris, Del (coach), 86
Haskell Institute, 107
Havlicek, John (Boston Celtics), 82–83, 83, 88, 91, 94
    NBA All-Star Games, 96
Hawkins, Hersey (Philadelphia 76ers), 49–50
Hayes, Elvin, 60, 102, 102, 105
Hazzard, Walt (Los Angeles Lakers), 91, 118
Heinsohn, Tom (Boston Celtics), 79, 91
Helms National Championship, 107, 109
Henefeld, Nadav, 12
Higgins, Rod (Golden State Warriors), 96
Hodges, Craig (Chicago Bulls), 95
Holy Cross College, 77
Hoosier Dome (Indiana), 8, 10
Hoosiers (movie), 11
Houston Astrodome, 103
Houston Rockets, 14, 65, 95
Houston, Kevin, 100
Hunt, Anderson, 116
Hurley, Bobby, 115

**I**

Iba, Henry (coach), 106, 110, 116
Indiana, basketball in, 8, 9–11, 9, 10, 11, 109
    Indiana Basketball Hall of Fame, 11, 11
    Indiana University, 42, 106, 111, 116, 119

**J**

Japan, basketball in, 11–12, 34
Johnson, Dennis, 88
Johnson, Earvin "Magic," (Los Angeles Lakers), 13, 14, 26, 34, 34, 38–42, 39
    assists, 26–27, 40

Most Valuable Player, 38, 58
    NBA All-Star Games, 96
    rebounds, 40
Johnson, Kevin (Phoenix Suns), 14, 41–42, 42, 95–96
Johnson, Larry, 64, 116, 120
Johnson, Marques, 118
Johnson, Vinnie "The Microwave" (Detroit Pistons), 49
Johnston, Neil, 78
Jones, Bobby, 95
Jones, K.C. (Boston Celtics), 91
Jones, Sam (Boston Celtics), 88, 91
Jordan, Michael (Chicago Bulls), 13, 14, 15, 21, 34, 34, 41, 44–46, 44, 45, 46, 54, 91, 110, 118
    NBA All-Star Games, 96

**K**

Kautsky Grocers (Indianapolis), 109
Kaze, Irv (CBA Commissioner), 96
Kemp, Shawn, 95
Keogan, George (coach), 108
Kersey, Jerome (Portland Trail Blazers), 60
King, Bernard, 50–51, 50
Knickerbocker Arena (Albany), 96
Knight, Bobby (coach), 41, 58, 106, 110–111, 111
Krzyzewski, Mike (coach), 116
Kundlas, John (coach), 91

**L**

Laettner, Christian, 115
Laimbeer, Bill (Detroit Pistons), 70, 70
Lemon, Meadowlark, 35
Lever, Lafayette, 49
Lewis, Guy (coach), 103, 119
Lincoln College (Illinois), 96
Los Angeles Clippers, 100, 106
Los Angeles Lakers, 12, 13, 21, 38, 40, 55, 82, 88. See also Minneapolis Lakers.
    NBA championship series, 91, 94, 95
Los Angeles Times, 41
Loughery, Kevin (coach), 51
Louisiana State University, 78, 103
Louisiana Superdome, 118
Louisiana Tech, 58
Lovellette, Clyde (Minneapolis Lakers), 78
Lucas, Jerry, 83
Luisetti, Angelo "Hank" (Stanford University), 22
Lynam, Jim (coach), 59

**M**

Macauley, Ed, 88
Malone, Karl (Utah Jazz), 14, 22, 34, 34, 58, 59
    NBA All-Star Games, 96
Malone, Moses (Atlanta Hawks), 22, 23, 46, 58, 71
    Most Valuable Player, 38
Manning, Danny, 34, 100, 105–106, 106
Maravich, Pete 103–104, 104
Marciulionis, Saronas (Golden State Warriors), 12
Marion Giants (high school team), 9–10
McCarthy, Joe, 88
McDaniel, Xavier (Phoenix Suns), 57, 73
McDonald's Open, 12
McGinnis, George, 10
McGuire, Frank (coach), 91, 110
McHale, Kevin (Boston Celtics), 54, 60, 61, 88
    injury, 60
McNeese State University (Louisiana), 47
Meadowlands Stadium (New Jersey), 114
Memphis State University, 105
Meyer, Ray (coach), 76, 106, 108
Meyers, Dave, 86, 118
Miami Heat, 13
Michigan State University, 38, 54
Mikan, George, 62, 76–77, 76, 91
Miller, Cheryl, 27, 49
Miller, Reggie (Indiana), 49
Milwaukee Bucks, 86, 101
    NBA championship series, 94
Minneapolis Lakers, 35, 62, 76–77, 79–80, 91.
    See also Los Angeles Lakers.
    NBA championship series, 91
Moe, Doug (coach), 49
Mourning, Alonzo (Charlotte Hornets), 65
Mullin, Chris (Golden State Warriors), 55, 57
Murphy, Calvin, 28
Murphy, Tod, 96
Murray, Jim (columnist), 41

**N**

Naismith, Dr. James, 11, 14, 16, 17–19, 27, 107
Nance, Larry (Phoenix Suns), 60
National Association of Basketball Coaches, 107
National Basketball Association (NBA), 11, 12, 13, 84
    NBA All-Star Games, 95–96
    NBA championship series, 91, 94–95
National Basketball League (NBL), 76
National Collegiate Athletic Association (NCAA), 14, 27
    NCAA Tournament, 107, 114–116, 118–119, 108, 119
National Invitation Tournament (NIT), 27, 76, 77, 108
NBC Sports, 14
Neal, Curly, 35
Nelson, Don, 58, 65, 91
Nevitt, Chuck, 31, 34
New Jersey Nets, 51, 60, 96
New Orleans Jazz, 104

New York Knicks, 12, 13, 51, 62, 72, 88, 102
    NBA championship series, 94
New York Nets, 85
New York Times, 11, 19
Newell, Pete (coach), 106–107
Newlin, Ron (curator of Indiana Basketball Hall of Fame), 11
Nicholson, Jack, 13
North Carolina State University, 118, 119
Notre Dame University, 100, 108

**O**

Oakley, Charles (New York Knicks), 46, 60, 62, 74
Ohio State University, 82, 83, 110, 116
Oklahoma State University, 108, 116
Olajuwon, Hakeem (Houston Rockets), 14, 47, 65, 69, 70–71, 119
Olympics and basketball, 11, 12, 14, 34, 57, 58, 82, 102, 107, 111
Oxford University, 102

**P**

Paddio, Gerald, 12
Paint, the, 58
Pan-American Games, 82, 111
Parrish, Robert (Boston Celtics), 54, 72, 88
Paspalj, Zarko (San Antonio), 12
Paxson, John (Chicago Bulls), 44
Perkins, Sam, 118
Perry, William "The Refrigerator," 14
Petrovic, Drazen (Portland Trail Blazers), 12
Pettit, Robert Lee Jr. (St. Louis Hawks), 77–78
    NBA All-Star Games, 96
Philadelphia 76ers, 14, 31, 58–59, 62, 90
    NBA championship series, 91, 94
Phoenix Suns, 14, 41–42, 57
Pippen, Scottie (Chicago Bulls), 34, 34, 57, 74
Point guard
    Cousy, Bob, 27, 28, 40, 70, 77, 80, 86, 91, 96
    definition, 37
    importance of, 40
    Johnson, Earvin "Magic," 13, 14, 26–27, 26, 38–42, 39, 58, 96
    Johnson, Kevin, 14, 41–42, 42, 95–96
    Price, Mark, 42
    protection of ball, 41
    Stockton, John, 14, 28, 40–41, 40
    Thomas, Isiah, 13, 41, 42, 43, 95, 96
Porter, Kevin, 28
Porter, Terry (Portland Trail Blazers), 47, 60, 95
Portland Trail Blazers, 12, 22, 47, 60, 96
    NBA championship series, 94, 95
Power forward
    Barkley, Charles, 14, 36, 58–60, 61
    definition, 37

Hayes, Elvin, 60, 102, *102*, 105
 Malone, Karl, 14, *22*, 58, *59*, 96
 Oakley, Charles, 46, 60, 62, *74*
 Williams, Buck, 22, 47, 60, *62*
Price, Mark (Cleveland Cavaliers), 42
Princeton University, 101, 102
Professional Basketball Writers of America, 79
Providence University, 112
Purdue University, 109

**Q**

Quad City Thunder, 96

**R**

Rambis, Kurt, 34
Ramsey, Frank (Boston Celtics), 91
Rebound, the, 22, 58, 60
Reed, Willis, 65
Riley, Pat (coach), 38, 86, 88, *89*
Rizzuto, Phil, 88
Robertson, Oscar, 26, 28, 38, 40, 41, 76,
 100–101, 105
 NBA All-Star Games, 95, 96
Robinson, David (San Antonio Spurs), 14, *29*,
 34, 42, 65, 68, *68*, 70
Robinson, Rumeal, 119
Rodman, Dennis (Detroit Pistons), *74*, 91
Roundfield, Dan, 95
Rucker League, 84
Rupp, Adolph (coach), 91, 106, 107–108, *108*
Russell, Bill (Boston Celtics), 62, 64, 76, 79,
 *78*, 88, 91, 94, 118
 Most Valuable Player, 38, 79
 rebounds, 22

**S**

Salaries (players), 13
Sampson, Ralph, 65
San Antonio Spurs, 42, 65, 68, 70, 96
San Diego Rockets, 60
Saperstein, Abe, 35
Schayes, Dolph, 78
School for Christian Workers (Springfield,
 Massachusetts), *18*
Scott, Byron (Los Angeles Lakers), *21*
Scott, Dr. Norman, 51
Seattle Mariners, 115
Seikaly, Ron (Miami Heat), 72
Selvy, Frank, 100
Seton Hall University, 12
Shaker, Ted (CBS Sports), 13
Share, Charlie, 77

Sharman, Bill (Boston Celtics), 28, 79, 88, 91
Shaw, Brian, 12
Shooting guard
 definition, 37
 Drexler, Clyde, 47, *52*, 60, *97*
 Dumars III, Joe, 47, 49, *49*
 English, Alex, 57
 Harper, Ron, 49–50
 Hawkins, Hersey, 49–50
 Johnson, Vinnie, 49
 Jordan, Michael, 13, 14, *15*, 21, *34*, 41,
 44–46, *44*, *45*, *46*, 54, 96, 110, 118
 Lever, Lafayette, 49
 Miller, Reggie, *48*, 49
Siegfried, Larry, 83
Skiles, Scott (Orlando Magic), 28
Skyhook, the, 85, 86
Slam dunk, 19, 28, 30, 70, 95
Small forward
 Bird, Larry, 11, 13, 14, *20*, 51, 54, *55*, 88,
 *92–93*
 Chambers, Tom, 11–12, *56*, 57, 96
 definition, 37
 Erving, Julius, 14, *17*, *21*, 47, 51, 77, 84–85,
 *84*, 95, 96
 kinds of, 50
 King, Bernard, 50–51, *50*
 McDaniel, Xavier, 57
 Mullin, Chris, 55, 57
 Wilkins, Jacques, 54–55, *56*
 Worthy, James, 38, 55, *57*, 118
Smart, Keith, 119
Smith, Dean (coach), 106, 110, *117*
Smith, Elmore, 86
St. Louis Hawks, 77, 88
 NBA championship series, 91, 94
Stagg, Amos Alonzo, 19
Steitz, Ed, 21
Stern, David (NBA Commissioner), 11, 12, 13
Stockton, John (Utah Jazz), 14, 28, 40–41, *40*
 assists, 41
Sullivan Award, 102

**T**

Tarkanian, Jerry, 108, 116
Television and basketball, 13–14
Thomas, Isiah (Detroit Pistons), 13, 41, 42,
 *43*, 95
 NBA All-Star Games, 96
Thompson, David, 95
Thompson, John (coach), 34, 72, 106, 112,
 *113*, 114
Three-second rule, 19
Tri-City Hawks, 77, 87
Triple-double, the, 40, 44
Turner, Todd, 115
Twenty-four-second clock, 19

**U**

United States Basketball League, 31
University of California at Los Angeles
 (UCLA), 10, 86, 100, 103, 104, 105, 106,
 110, 118
University of Cincinnati, 76, 101, 118
University of Connecticut, 114, 115
University of Georgia, 54
University of Houston, 47, 103
University of Iowa, 96
University of Kansas, 62, 80, 105, 106, 107
University of Kentucky, 106, 107, 116
University of Louisville, 112
University of Maryland, 60
University of Massachusetts, 84
University of Michigan, 119
University of Minnesota, 60
University of Nevada at Las Vegas (UNLV),
 115, 116
University of North Carolina, 46, 106, 110, 118
University of Pennsylvania, 90
University of San Francisco, 62, 76, 79, 118
Utah Jazz, 11, 14, 28, 58, 41

**V**

Vance, Gene, 77
Villanova University, *99*, *118*, 119
Virginia Union University, 62
Volkov, Alexander (Atlanta Hawks), 12

**W**

Wagner, Milt, 12
Walker, Darrell (Washington Bullets), 49
Walton, Bill, 70, 100, 105, 118
Walton, Bruce, 105
Washington Bullets, 31, 51
Washington Capitols, 87
Webb, Anthony Jerome "Spud" (Atlanta
 Hawks), 31, *32–33*
Wesley, Walt, 86
West Virginia University, 80
West, Jerry (Los Angeles Lakers), 21, 22, 44,
 80, 82, *82*, 91, 94, 105
Westhead, Paul (coach), 88
Westphal, Paul (Boston Celtics), 88
White, Jo Jo (Boston Celtics), 88
Whittenburg, Derrick, 119
Wichita State University, 57
Wicks, Sidney, 110, 118
Wilkes, Keith, 118
Wilkins, Jacques Dominique (Atlanta Hawks),
 28, *36*, 54–55, *56*
Williams, Buck (Portland Trail Blazers), 22,
 47, 60, *62*

Williams, John "Hot Rod," 13, *13*
Winston-Salem College, 107
Winters, Brian, 86
Wooden, John (coach), 10, 14, 30, 103, 105,
 109–110, *109*, 118
Woodward, Lynette, 35
Worthy, James (Los Angeles Lakers), 38, 55,
 *57*, 118

**Z**

Zaslovsky, Max, 76